ULRICH ROESCH
many, close to the Swi
studies in philosophy, ḻ
and social sciences. From 1971 he worked at the International Cultural Centre in Achberg, Lindau, Germany, at the Institute for Social Development Research, where his research work focused chiefly on alternative forms of economy, and organizational development. He collaborated with fellow researchers, professors Leif Holbaek-Hanssen, Ota Sik, Eugen Loebl, Joseph Beuys, Wilfried Heidt and Wilhelm Schmundt. He is now a member of the executive board, and lectures at several colleges and universities.

In 1976, he co-founded the Waldorf School in Wangen, in the Allgäu district and worked as its Principal. In 1982, with his wife Cornelia, he established a textile company that manufactures garments using organically cultivated cotton in social projects in India. In 2012 he helped establish the school for biodynamic agriculture in Vinobajipuram, Tamil Nadu, South India. From 1999 to 2011, he worked at the Goetheanum's Section for Social Sciences in Dornach, Switzerland, and lectured on the 'Social Sculpture' course in Wangen, Achberg, Germany.

His publications include: 'Von der Sozialwissenschaft zur Sozialen Kunst' ('From social science to social art'), in *Die Kunst des sozialen Bauens*, Wangen 1993; *Eine andere Welt ist möglich—mehr gute Ideen zur Globalisierung* ('Another world is possible—elements for a post-materialistic understanding of globalization'), Vienna 2003; and 'An Overview of Joseph Beuys's concepts of money and capital' in *What is Money?*, Sussex 2010. He is also editor of and contributor to *Vision and Action for Another World. Powerful ideas and inspiring practical approaches*, Kolkata 2004.

WE ARE THE REVOLUTION!

Rudolf Steiner, Joseph Beuys and the Threefold Social Impulse

ULRICH ROESCH

TEMPLE LODGE

Temple Lodge Publishing
Hillside House, The Square
Forest Row, RH18 5ES

www.templelodge.com

Published by Temple Lodge 2013

© Ulrich Roesch 2013

The moral right of the author has been asserted under the Copyright, Designs and Patents Act, 1988

With thanks to Peter Schata and Alexandra Umbreit for use of illustrations. Every effort has been made to identify copyright holders. The publishers will be happy to correct any omissions in future editions

All rights reserved. No part of this publication may be reproduced, stored in a retrieval system, or transmitted, in any form or by any means, electronic, mechanical, photocopying or otherwise, without the prior permission of the publishers

A catalogue record for this book is available from the British Library

ISBN 978 1 906999 52 0

Cover by Morgan Creative featuring image of Joseph Beuys by kind permission of Alexandra Umbreit
Typeset by DP Photosetting, Neath, West Glamorgan
Printed and bound in the UK by 4edge Ltd, Essex

Contents

Foreword by Michael Lapointe	1
1. The Threefold Social Organism (2013)	7
2. 'We are the Revolution' (Beuys): Individuality as the Nucleus of Social Transformation (2009)	14
3. Just Bananas ... The Social Organism as a Work of Art (2008)	24
4. Spirituality and Social Action: Mahatma Gandhi and Rudolf Steiner (2008)	31
5. 'We Create Social Conditions.' The Contemporary Relevance of Rudolf Steiner's Social Concepts (2005)	50
6. The Middle Realm of Social Life—the Rights Sphere as Our Earthly Task (2010)	63
7. Rudolf Steiner's World Economy and the Goethean Research Method (2011)	67
8. The Biodynamic Farm and the Social Organism (2012)	75

Dedication and thanks

This book is dedicated to my friends in Taiwan, who helped this project happen: Dr. Yi-Ling Chang (who made the whole venture possible), Jack Yang and his wife Christine Chen (who hosted me), Ruo-Jun Yu (my wonderful translator), Exun Hsieh (teacher at the school, who drove me safely to the venue), Cheng-Ci Lee (who accompanied me to the airport and gave worthy insights into Taiwanese culture), Lydia Chang (who helped me to understand Taiwanese history and religion), Dr. Chia-Lung Lin (legislator in the Taiwanese Parliament) and his wife Wan-Ru Liao (who initiated several ad-hoc 'summit talks'), Shy-Tyng Kai and her daughter, Hsin-Shih Lai (the excellent eurythmy performer and teacher), Alexandra Chen, and all the other brothers and sisters whom I met at the conference. Thanks to them, a Chinese edition of this book will be published simultaneously in Taiwan.

Thanks to Hans von Florenstein Mulder, who, as the person responsible for the Asia-Pacific region, prepared the anthroposophical conference, and invited me to come to Taiwan.

Thanks to my collaborator in the US, Michael Lapointe, who, besides being a translator and editor, is also a partner in developing healing social concepts for the future.

Last but not least thanks to Sevak E. Gulbekian, chief editor of Temple Lodge Publishing, and his skilled editor Matthew Barton who worked hard to improve the readability of my texts in English.

Ulrich Roesch

Foreword

Why should you be interested in this collection of essays by Ulrich Roesch, and what is a productive way to meet this work? This is my directing question here. As a researcher and writer, Ulrich is steeped in the deepest social questions: money, economy and the question of how to change humanity's course, including insight into the spiritual realm. It is rare, especially if you look at the sheer volume of what is written today on social questions, for writers to focus on the spiritual nature of the human being as a key aspect. It is perhaps rarer still for a social scientist and spiritual scientist to cultivate such a close relationship with the artistic realm. This is one reason why his volume of essays is important. I share with the author a great appreciation for the work and person of Joseph Beuys, and it is partly this that makes it such a pleasure for me to introduce Ulrich's work to you.

Like many who will read this book, I have spent my life committed to penetrating the riddles of our human existence in a practical way, engaging especially with the mysteries of spirit—a task that our modern scientific community seems to brush off too easily by relegating it to spheres of faith. If you are reading this, then I suspect you understand me when I say that I am not satisfied with this situation. I now know that if a person works for it, then real wisdom can be found, with deep and penetrating insights into life. Even discovering how much we don't know is a vital insight. To bring health to our social life, we must gain full understanding of the human being, and therefore cultivate a picture of where we stand in our development today, where we are coming from, and form a real sense of where we are heading. Such a picture is precisely what is lacking in almost every book by contemporary social theorists. Studying the work of those who draw on spiritual insights is a legitimate, even necessary path towards gaining the same capacities ourselves. This is what many have found with the person and work of Rudolf Steiner, along with a handful of others, such as Sri Aurobindo and Paramahansa Yogananda, whose ideas support and weave through Ulrich Roesch's work. If humanity is to have a future worthy of the name, spiritual questions must be included in our scientific progress. Ulrich understands this clearly, and it has been a pleasure to be able to work with him, hear him speak, and help him edit and translate some of the essays in this book.

Modern scientists rely upon human cognition, which is a spiritual process supported by a healthy brain, and not simply an electro-chemical process; yet most scientists fail to recognize it as such. Ulrich's work encompasses the broader context of the human being, our spiritual development, the role of reincarnation and karma, and the reality of spirit in our cognitive process. In his essay on the biodynamic farm and the social organism (Chapter 8), Ulrich gives the following quote by Rudolf Steiner:

> The course of a human life within the framework of life and death is determined in three different ways, and we are therefore also dependent on three factors that go beyond birth and death. The body is subject to the laws of heredity; the soul is subject to self-created destiny or, to use an ancient term, to its karma; and the spirit is subject to the laws of reincarnation, or repeated earthly lives

Where is this understanding, which we so surely require, to be found in all the popular books circulating today? What is the consequence of its absence in all the thought prevailing today?

I consider it vital to highlight four aspects as part of this foreword. Firstly, there is often a gap between the words and ideas we learn from others and our own insights and knowledge that we develop through *intuitive thinking*. Secondly, we are faced by a social task that cannot be accomplished by one person alone; it must be achieved by many individuals working together if it is to have meaning for all. Thirdly, we ourselves determine our future, so as to become self-actualized adults in spiritual terms, in short: artists creating themselves and the future world. Fourthly, the gap between knowledge and action is something that needs to be overcome: how do we make our insights fruitful in practical terms?

Intuitive thinking

Understanding what is meant by *intutitive thinking*, and coming to experience it, is essential to the tasks modern science faces today. Intuitive thinking is a faculty that awakens within us as we develop, as we progress to a certain level of mature cognitive capacity, but it only does so if we school it in the right way. This is something whose first stages I only began to experience after the age of 42. We can overlook this and fail to recognize it if we do not apply ourselves to its development. And as Ulrich will show, each person's cognitive process is individual, and the way we compose our own pictures of life deserves to be called artistic. Ulrich addresses this topic when he speaks of the Goethean method of research, especially in Chapter 7. This is also the method whereby we develop the faculty of intuitive thinking itself. Ulrich makes us aware of the methodology, and then he asks us to use it, to develop a pictorial consciousness in order to study the phenomena he addresses. If there is a difficulty in his works, it is that of balancing the scope of any essay's topic with enough detail for the reader to experience all the essentials points. This is why Ulrich reiterates that what he presents offers only signposts—there is a much bigger and richer picture that could be developed, and will unfold, for those who themselves pursue the path in depth. Ulrich Roesch's work is full of hard-won insights. He makes us aware that what he is offering is also what he himself has had to discover in his own search: which is to engage with the key signposts until they lead to individual experiences of knowledge and understanding.

Rudolf Steiner often highlighted the need to discern the essential from the non-essential, using the method described so well by Goethe. A number of contemporary researchers and writers have succeeded in describing the process of thinking in progressive stages as these arise from direct observation of studied phenomena. We can find important examples for our own social understanding when we study those who use this method today, such as Ulrich Roesch and others he has worked with. As a young man Ulrich studied and worked with Joseph Beuys and Wilhelm Schmundt, accomplished thinkers and strong personalities. Later he worked with contemporaries such as Claus Otto Scharmer and colleagues at MIT in Boston. The latter is developing Theory U, an in-depth mode of phenomenological study and awareness of group process that can illuminate all aspects of planning and problem-solving, and is vital in the transformation of economic life. Ulrich has also collaborated with two colleagues of mine from upstate NY, who founded The Center for Social Research. These are Christopher Schaefer and Gary Lamb, working respectively on research into income inequalities—a pressing rights question in our time—and freedom for education and funding processes as essential to proper development of the cultural life. Each of these individuals offers substance for engaging with important social questions.

I would also mention here Tom Atlee in the US, who has undertaken important international socio-political research on the processes and understanding involved in developing collaborative public insights and initiatives; and Zvi Szir's artistic, philosophical and anthroposophical research in Switzerland. Tom Atlee's 2012 book *Empowering Public Wisdom: A Practical Vision of Citizen-Led Politics* is exemplary in clarity and methodology—essentially using the Goethean Method, as does Ulrich. Zvi Szir is an artist and teacher, co-founder of the New Art School in

Basel, Switzerland, whose extensive practice and research in art and art history, philosophy and anthroposophy culminate in one of the finest examples I have witnessed of phenomenological, intuitive thinking. His recent articles on art history and his newest series, exploring some of the most important philosophers writing since the year 2000, have appeared over the past year in German in *Das Goetheanum* magazine, and are worth seeking out. It was through Zvi that I came to a deep experience of art, Joseph Beuys included, and found help in bringing the most challenging ideas down into experiential, tangible form.

Working with others

Our path of personal development starts close to home, to improve our own lives and our own understanding. We start by learning from others and we progress to a very critical point, when two things are realized. First, we realize that we accomplish far less alone, and secondly that what we accomplish will have most meaning if we change things for the benefit of all. Ulrich understands this. In Chapter 3 he attempts to bring into focus the task that faces us if we seriously wish to understand how we are connected to the lives of individuals elsewhere in the world. We can no longer afford to concern ourselves only with ourselves. In this essay, Ulrich looks at global banana production and distribution as a good way of studying processes we are involved in that happen far away from us in geography and awareness. He doesn't miss an opportunity for well-placed humour here, and I laughed out loud when reading it. Our lives are much more complex today than ever before. Our interactions in the marketplace, and the ways we spend our so-called free time, have changed dramatically in the past decades. We are more anti-social than ever, more enclosed in our own personal worlds. This requires an effort from us all. We see here that thinking alone is not enough, but that feeling and action are also vital, as the discourse on bananas fully elaborates.

Becoming truly human

Intrinsic to our current stage of evolution is that we must now become masters of our own destiny: we can each strive to realize our inner potential and actively do what is right rather than being merely a recipient and consumer. We must become *true human beings*. What is our picture of a true human being? We must each become a self-regulating, self-creating individual—something more than we are now. But self-realization is not achieved alone. As modern people, we no longer work just for ourselves, and nor should we. We have our needs met by others and our work goes to meet the needs of others. We must mature to become true human beings, and also a true humanity in general. If we want to understand Ulrich Roesch, we must pay close attention to how this concept of a true human being relates to the full dimensions of what it means to be an artist.

Rudolf Steiner often spoke about how humanity stands at the threshold. What is this threshold? Something is asked of us, both as individuals and in human community. As individuals we awaken to a true experience of our higher I-consciousness, our spiritual self. We learn who we are, and work to embrace and realize the whole of our nature, to make it our own, and then to create our future selves out of our own capacities, in co-creation with others in the world. As a whole humanity, we mature to become co-creators of our own society and stewards of all the earth: a spiritual, living, self-creating social organism—made up of many self-actualized individuals, each generating wisdom in self-determining and co-creating collaboration. The lives we develop together become a collectively created social work of art; or to use Ulrich's words: a social sculpture. Everywhere in these essays, we can find presented the principles we need in order to understand our present and future: human social life in its threefold nature—of economic fraternity, rights equality, and freedom in cultural life; and the fundamental social law that shows us how we can relate to each other to make society healthy. These are insights that arise from clear observation of life. But they can only fulfil their task if people do their own study and research and, most importantly, engage their will as Ulrich's essays can encourage us to do.

We need to grow beyond the abstract ideas that we assimilate unthinkingly from our current consumer culture—ideas we absorb by imitation. We can grow into ideas full of life and vitality that we generate out of our own activity, by observing life and the living world of thought pictures that are waiting to reveal themselves if we are attentive. We can commit ourselves to learning, caring, and acting together. Much work needs to be done, and it is my hope that this book of essays will act as a stimulus not just to the casual thinking of the curious, but to the concentrated attention of those who seek real knowledge and wisdom and are committed to basing fruitful actions on hard-won insights.

The gap between knowledge and action
There is a gap between knowledge and action, which is also the gap between knowledge and *wisdom*, and we do well to mind the gap. Our process of learning is such that we learn both through study and through doing; study without doing will prove inadequate. Our doing involves

both physical actions and our own efforts in thinking. Real thinking and philosophizing involve an act of will. In the social sphere, learning from and engaging in collaborative action is essential, and this action can bring us directly into the artistic sphere—which is the truly human sphere. Our starting point is often found in the hard-won experiences of those preceding us. Ulrich rightly calls these: signposts and hints. It is up to us the readers to give these signposts enough attention, effort and depth of consideration, to allow our experiences to act upon us, and lead us to action. This book is itself a result of Ulrich's research in many of the hot spots of social change in the world. But it will only fulfil its task if people do their own study and research, preliminary to their own actions. *Vision and Action* was the title of a previous book that Ulrich published in Calcutta, India. We can hope that this wish for vision and action will become reality: that people all over the world start walking their own path of inner social development so that this in turn works fruitfully to shape society.

Michael Lapointe
Spring solstice, 21 March 2013

1. The Threefold Social Organism

Freedom for the spiritual-cultural life, equality and democracy for the rights life, initiative and solidarity for economic life

The social issues of the 21st century should be considered against the background of a now global dimension. The time of small national entities is over. We are living in a globalized world. Our world has become one through our mutual dependence and global division of labour. Rudolf Steiner mentioned this in his economic course:

> What one could compare individual countries to, at the most, would be cells of an organism; as an economic body, the entire world can only be compared to an organism. We have to take note of this. Ever since we have had a world economy, it is much easier to understand that individual countries can only be compared to cells. The whole Earth considered as an economic organism, is the (actual) social organism ...[1]

We have to learn that people all over the world are our brothers and sisters, with different skin colours and maybe also different thoughts and consciousness, and different feelings. This makes our task difficult, but also very exciting and rich. So let's try to live consciously in our new, unified world!

The global dimension of our economic life is understood by our fellow citizens today. But to understand what 'social' means might be much more difficult. In the past, the word 'social' made one think of being charitable, giving alms, putting a coin in the poor box for paupers. What does the word mean to us today? Rudolf Steiner uses the word 'community' (*Gemeinschaft*) to refer to a social entity. He says:

> In a community of human beings working together, the wellbeing of the community will be the greater, the less the individual claims for himself the proceeds of the work he himself has done; i.e. the more of these proceeds he gives over to his fellow workers, and the more his own requirements are satisfied, not out of his work, but out of work done by the others.

Steiner calls this a fundamental social law.

If we look at a community of human beings working together, first we see a group of workers. Such groups have developed out of small medieval craftsman communities. Our view of 'working together' today immediately widens to encompass large national enterprises and corporations. And today's realities further expand to include transnational companies and groups. In the age of globalization, it has become ever more obvious that communities of human beings working together have to be understood globally. The fundamental social law only finds its living expression in actual reality, 'when a community of human beings succeeds in creating institutions where the results (of all work) wholly benefit the community'. In our times, social actions will only have a health-giving effect if activists are mindful of all their sisters and brothers, all over the world. It is very clear that every group has to find its own way, its own solutions. But we all have to keep the whole of humanity in mind.

Rudolf Steiner described the shape of modern society as a threefold social organism. During a course in Breslau-Koberwitz on 17 June 1924, Steiner spoke of threefolding as necessarily rooted in the nature of the human being, and as a vital social impulse. This book seeks to explore possible ways to understand this and to work towards a healthy social future.

Being a social activist (whether as teachers, parents in a Waldorf School, biodynamic farmers, physicians etc.) we have to be aware of this threefold form. We need to study it and find a lively inner picture for this new social reality without imposing external schemas on it. Such a picture of threefolding only gives us a background, a context that has to inform our social activity. But no single one of us alone can fulfil the needs of our time. Many people have to come together. This again is what makes our times so hard and complex, but also so rich and full of potential.

Of course, different social groups will always have to do things in their own way. What is right for one group might be totally wrong for another. Each has to find its own solutions. To do this in a modern, healthy way, we have to act out of consciousness for the whole of humanity and the earth.

The threefold social organism—a phenomenological approach to social issues. How can we experience a spiritual reality in the given social world?

Steiner describes the task for economists as well as for social scientists thus: phenomena appearing in the world are to be understood by insight-oriented thinking. He developed his ideas out of his experience of modern industrial society as it exists in the context of liberal capitalism, experiencing that the social organism is shaped in a threefold manner.

Interestingly, it was in the course of his observations of fundamental social forms that Steiner perceived that our modern society, which had grown asocial, has a seed of true 'socialism' hidden within it for all-embracing fraternity and co-existence. In fact, industrial society itself actually demands selfless activity from people, to work for one another. Liberal ideology, which furthers egotism in all our social relationships, is opposed to this—and this impacts on our contemporary society in a problematic way.

When speaking of the fundamental social law, Rudolf Steiner emphasized that 'working for one's fellow men, and the aim of earning an income, of whatever amount, must be kept separate'.

Twelve years after formulating this fundamental law, Steiner discovered the phenomenon of the threefold organism in the human being and in the social realm. He articulated it thus: Freedom and individualism for the spiritual life, democracy for the life of rights, and solidarity for the economic life.

Steiner had developed the concept of a globalized economy as early as the 1920s. The key to fraternal collaboration lies in the division of labour. Every person who is economically active produces something for the requirements of others. Others ensure that he can live in dignity by producing food, clothing, housing etc. for him. This is solidarity, interdependence, give and take.

The result of recognizing these facts is to come to a totally new approach to economic processes. Steiner's concept for an industrial society and for a post-industrial economy attempts to unite free people whose initiative arises out of a principle of economic solidarity. He explains the form of an associative economic life in which free initiative and fraternal elements are brought together in a creative form. The main problem is the seeming opposition between the interests of producers and consumers. A new social form is required to bridge this polarity.

Obviously in such an association, consumers' interests should be equally represented alongside those of experienced and professional producers. It is obvious too that all obligations resulting from legal considerations, such as environmental protection, should also be present in such an organization.

These types of social associations should be formed regionally. Their members should be entrepreneurs from all fields: vertical as well as horizontal collaboration should occur. It is obvious that cultural institutions are also to be represented in such associations. A direct merger of economic and cultural institutions would result in new forms of financing which could bypass the cost-intensive route via the State.

Surpluses could then flow directly to cultural institutions. Other types of communal tasks could be financed through direct taxation on expenditure. Exemption should apply to all indirect taxes, or taxes that would result in increased labour costs. In fact there is already quite a strong movement in Europe for 'a basic income, and an expenditure tax' headed by Götz Werner and Benediktus Hardorp, both from Germany.

Associations should be attached to institutions resembling banks, with the task of translating into action whatever is recognized as the right thing to do. The granting of credit by these banks should also be governed by the association's decisions. Rudolf Steiner viewed the founding of such 'associative banks' as particularly vital.

As social scientists we can experience the social organism as an inner spiritual picture, but then we have to become artists when we act socially. For the artist then creates a new, unique piece of art out of the archetype. This is also the process we have to follow in the social realm. In doing so, within a free community, we move from social science to *social art*.

The founding of the Waldorf School from the movement for a threefold social order

At the end of the First World War Rudolf Steiner talked to many leading figures in the political realm. But they were not ready to embrace new ideas or to pursue new avenues, so social breakdown continued and revolutionary groups arose in all European countries. It was then that entrepreneurs from southern Germany came to Steiner and asked him to contribute something for the healing of the social organism. Steiner came and spoke to most of the larger companies, both to the workforces and also to the industrialists.

After initial success, political parties on both left and right opposed the threefold social order impulse—and the masses chose to follow their political leaders. Steiner took a practical step by launching the first Waldorf School with the collaboration of the directors and workers of the Waldorf Astoria cigarette factory. It was also meant to serve as an example for an institution born from free spiritual life, eliciting a response from all around the world—but this only happened 50 years later.

Steiner also helped start a new (profit-sharing) business enterprise called 'The Coming Day' where a new form of collaboration was sought whereby cultural enterprises such as the Waldorf School or the Goetheanum could be funded by the 'commonwealth's' economic enterprises.

Steiner also gave the Anthroposophical Society and movement a new social form. But he died before this could be fully accomplished. And his followers were unable to continue this great deed. Today this remains our task—not only in Europe, but in the whole world.

'Seven social processes and organs in a modern enterprise'— social organs and structures in a Waldorf School

Of course, the threefold concept also encompasses the primary structure of an enterprise—both in the cultural and the economic realms. The human body is also threefold: the nerve system centred in the head, the rhythmic system centred in the middle (heart), and the metabolic system centred in the periphery (the limbs). Correspondingly, we have the threefold shape of our social system: Debating colleagues create the free spiritual life—where abilities are cultivated and developed. The rights life evolves between human beings. In its best expression, equal rights forms its basis—and will help create human dignity. In the economic life, we work for our fellow human beings. Cooperation and work in partnership is the aim for which we strive, and creates fraternity in economic life.

But beside our threefold human structure, we also have a sevenfold form, an organization of etheric forces. This sevenfoldness can be described to help us to understand how a school or a working group could be organized. The human body has seven chief organs; and the social life of any group working together will correspondingly build seven social organs to establish an adequate organization.

1. Where and how do we find and declare our objectives? A 'Council of Elders' could oversee the right direction for our enterprises.
2. Do we also look to the future of our enterprise? Are we a permanent learning community? Have we developed organs of learning?
3. Have we fully established our abilities to perform our tasks sufficiently? Who reviews our performance and helps us to develop our faculties?
4. Which constitutional (social) form is adequate for our community? Do we have an assembly of members as a democratic organ?
5. Will our earnings (financial income) be sufficient? Do we have proper management of our finances? Do we balance our tasks with our financial possibilities?
6. Are our products, and what we do, required? Do we have a social body for consumers (the parents in a school)? Are we aware of our influence in the social environment?

7. Who is willing to guarantee the realization of our mission? Do we have an adequate executive committee? Who accepts the responsibility or liability for our enterprises?

At the beginning of an enterprise (such as a school) not all social organs will be developed right away. But we have to take care that they are already present in our awareness.

Education as a force for social change

Freedom, equality and fraternity are the functioning principles of a modern society built on self-administration. They can only aspire to what is truly human when they correspond to our essential nature in a threefold manner: freedom in spiritual life, equality in the legal sphere and fraternity in economic life (Rudolf Steiner).

Only when a sufficiently large number of people with these new insights seek to shape the world accordingly, can our social relationships be healed. The revival and strong growth of the worldwide movement for a civil society may encourage us. 'Créativité au Pouvoir', *Creativity Coming into Power* was the slogan of the May Revolt in Paris in 1968. This battle cry is even more valid today. To recognize and realize social trends and social processes is one aspect of our task, while artistic and creative development of new social forms must join it. Then people of goodwill can collectively create another, better world, worthy of the human being.

We cannot hope to produce paradisiacal conditions, but we can tackle a host of disorders in our society to enable the social organism to develop in a healthy manner. All those who work to bring this about are fellow artists creating the social sculpture.

A child takes his first developmental steps by walking (standing upright), talking and thinking. These provide the basic foundation for all processes of human development. Correspondingly, the first seven-year cycle in a person's life organizes itself in these three stages: 1st stage, where the child devotes himself to the world with his bodily organization, experiencing his surroundings in undistanced immediacy; 2nd stage, where the child lives in unbounded imagination and explores the world through play; and a 3rd stage, that of readiness for formal schooling, where playing games that imitate real life tasks automatically leads to a capacity for the abstract. Through imitation and participation in activities, children learn in a manner appropriate to the first seven-year cycle.

To understand modern life we have to think in terms of metamorphosis. The forces developed throughout the first seven years will be transformed into forces enabling us to stand as adults in the social realm, to shape it individually through our emerging human freedom.

In the second seven-year cycle, a child needs the authority and the personality of his teacher. This will create forces in an adult that enable him to accept other humans beings in their own right, as they are. This is the basis for true democratic behaviour and understanding of the social world.

After puberty a young person must learn about the world intellectually. Developing our thinking enables us to understand what other great thinkers have said. The ability to form an opinion and make judgements should awaken in each one of us. This is also the age when we gain the ability to understand today's world through thought. Being able to take an interest in the whole world and its phenomena gives an adult the capacity to develop cosmopolitanism. The capacity for companionship with other human beings will be the foundation for fraternity to thrive in economic life.

Anthroposophy, on whose foundation Waldorf kindergartens and Wadorf schools are based, takes account of the transformation of these forces. The harmony, happiness, health and love given to the child are transformed in later life into strength to shape the world, so that alongside great technical advances, advances are also made in humanizing our social life. Thus the great ideals of freedom, equality and fraternity can come ever closer to being a social reality.

It is these ideals, and their practical realization, that this book seeks to explore.[2]

Notes

1. Rudolf Steiner: *World Economy*, Rudolf Steiner Press, London 1972, lecture 1, 24.7.1922.
2. Here I wish to thank Michael Spence for all the stimulating ideas he provided in his book *After Capitalism* (published by Remedium Kft., Nagykovácsi 2012). Although we use very different methods in researching principles of a humane society, I feel him to be a companion on the path towards finding appropriate forms of human collaboration and social development.

2. 'We Are the Revolution' (Joseph Beuys):

Individuality as the Nucleus of Social Transformation

Nowadays when people hear the word revolution they often feel a little uncomfortable. And perhaps this is justified because in the past revolutions have brought a lot of suffering to innocent people. However, revolutions are caused by the fact that necessary changes did not happen at the right time. In nature, something is always born out of something similar to itself. Stagnation, or resistance to change, blocks these necessary developments from evolving as they need to. This creates a situation in which a leap needs to be made—this has often resulted in a violent revolution. If we look at any organism we can see what happens when there is congestion: the organism must resist it, otherwise it will die. This is how Beuys regards a social organism in need of urgent changes to avoid complete collapse.

With his often repeated phrase, 'La rivoluzzione siamo Noi' (We are the revolution) Beuys points out that real transformation must evolve from the human being. Only the human being can be the source of transformation in the human and social realm. But a 'we' is also required, an agreement with others. In modern times the individual has to connect with others, in agreement. This can be the solid foundation for healthy forms of co-existence.

Our social existence is in deep crisis. The financial crisis is only a symptom. Everything calls for change. However, in the world today it is hard to act quickly and, as the saying goes, people are more comfortable with 'the devil they know'. Where can we find models for the future? We first need to find new imaginations of what our future could look like. We need visions. These new imaginations must arise from clear, deepened thinking that requires our will—thinking that is an activity, which touches upon the true essence of what we are searching for.

The concepts and ideas that form the basis for our visions of new social processes and organizations must not be made arbitrarily. First each individual needs to consciously and actively touch upon what seeks to emerge from the phenomena themselves. This is an indispensable condition for making our world a better place. Although this is already difficult enough to carry out, it is not sufficient. We also need a large enough group of people, to come into communication and action, so that the new vision can become effective.

There are two requirements for each individual working in the social realm. The first is that through thinking each of us has to find the essence—or the archetype—underlying social phenomena, and the second is that we have to become artists. A Goethean scientist observes a plant, seeking the eternal and natural laws behind (or within) the plant, which allow him to imagine (or to create) new plants that have not existed before but obey eternal laws. Likewise an artist then makes a new, unique piece of art out of the archetype he has intuited. This is the process we must also follow in the social realm. In doing so we move from social science to social art: that is, we work not only with the scientist within us but also the artist. Here we can become 'experimenters' as Beuys understands it. In my opinion Beuys is the most important social artist of our time. As I have already suggested, it is important to realize that this social, artistic process cannot be carried out by only one human being—it needs a community, a faculty, an association of free individuals. It is here that a social sculpture can and must grow, as a renewed—and in Beuys's terms extended—artistic process.

Thus we come to the social art: where human relations and organizations are the materials that the social artist works with and whose inner laws he seeks to know organically. The 'beautiful' artistic social form has to be created. The social abilities we develop and acquire are the social artist's craft. The ideas out of which we work rise from the inner laws of the social organism. This requires our artistic intuition to act with other human beings at the right time and in the right way. So the social organism or parts of it can appear as a work of art arising from the cooperation of free individuals. This does not mean creating a 'utopia' but instead it means transforming the world so that, in Schiller's words, 'the beautiful' nature of a real human society can emerge.

Thus the first political actions by Beuys accord completely with the democratic and threefold impulse, particularly in his exhibition at the 'Documenta' (1972) in Kassel. There Beuys exhibited his office for Direct Democracy for 100 days and patiently discussed with thousands of visitors the threefold social organism and the impulse of social sculpture. It is here that you see most clearly a connection with the new threefold movement in Germany.

Joseph Beuys was inspired to meet Wilhelm Schmundt after attending meetings with groups advocating threefolding. Schmundt was one of the most important Goethean scientists of the time and was also a member of the Goetheanum's School of Spiritual Science. After studying Schmundt's books, Beuys then met him personally at a conference in Achberg organized by Wilfried Heidt. Schmundt conducted independent research on the reality of the social organism. He was clearly a Platonist, who lived completely in his experienced ideas. Phenomenology not ideology was his principle. His primary publication, 'The Social Organism in its Shape of Freedom', was published by Herbert Witzenmann (leader of the Section for Social Science at the Goetheanum) as study material for people connected to the Goetheanum. Many committed anthroposophical social scientists found Schmundt's work too independent and not compatible with their own studies.

Beuys felt completely differently: from the very outset he understood Schmundt's view of Goetheanistic social science. Beuys admired him greatly as 'our great teacher' and ends a letter to 'my dear, admired Wilhelm Schmundt', with 'unfading love for you and your work, truly yours, Joseph Beuys.' In order to understand Beuys's work it is important to take into consideration this crucial meeting with Schmundt.

The social organism is always developing, changing and undergoing constant metamorphosis. Sometimes it moves slowly and at other times it takes sudden leaps. Our economic system has also developed in this way. The bartering economy evolved into a money economy and then into an economy of faculties (abilities). Production is based on human abilities and on working in broad, comprehensive collaboration. As Eugen Loebl has said, our economic life has developed into an 'integral system'.

Eugen Loebl was a very interesting individual. He became a communist as a young man. He was persecuted as a Jew. He flew to England and became a member of the Czechoslovakian government in exile in London. After 1945, this talented economist returned to Czechoslovakia and was rewarded with a post as First Deputy Minister of Commerce. But in 1948 he faced charges alongside Rudolf Slansky in a show trial which set out to sweep away the old Czech communist officials. Loebl and two of his companions were 'only' sentenced to life imprisonment whilst the other eleven, including Slansky, were hanged. Loebl served eleven years in prison, during five of which he was kept in solitary confinement.

He found it very difficult to understand what had happened to him and so he started having imaginary discussions with Karl Marx. He would say to Marx, 'Come on, we adhered to all your concepts and proposals but we did not create a better human society, in fact the opposite has happened: we created a system that is even more inhumane and cruel. What did we do wrong, or where do you think we went wrong? Or what did *you* think wrong?' He was only allowed to have the books of Marx and Lenin in prison. And paragraph by paragraph he studied Marx's chief works—including *Capital*. Remember he was condemned to a life in prison, so he had enough time! One of the problems he faced in these studies was being unable to write his findings on paper because, if the guard had found them, his sentence would have been lengthened and the conditions of his imprisonment would have changed for the worse. So he memorized all his ideas, concepts and findings by heart. After eleven years Loebl fell ill and was pardoned and released from prison. He immediately wrote down what he had discovered in his imaginary discussions with Karl Marx. The manuscript was smuggled to Vienna and printed as a book. The result of his research was also the title of his book *Geistige Arbeit* ('Spiritual work as the true source of common wealth').

Eugen Loebl was a communist and a materialist, yet his grounding in reality brought him to a deep spiritual knowledge of the social realm. Fifteen years later he was astonished to find that Rudolf Steiner had come to similar results through his own esoteric research.

Loebl became president of the state bank in Bratislava and was one of the promoters of the Prague Spring in 1968, in efforts to shape a new society. Because the leaders of the Soviet Republic did not want a socialist society based on freedom and democracy, the Russian tanks stopped this Czechoslovakian experiment. So Eugen Loebl had to go into exile again, this time becoming a professor at Vasar College in New York. He died in Manhattan at the age of 80, on 8 August 1987.

Back in 1974, Loebl had become a research fellow at the Institute for Social Research in Achberg—where I worked as a research assistant in the mid-seventies—where he also collaborated with Joseph Beuys and Ota Sik, the former Czech secretary of state (minister for the economy).

As Loebl stated, the modern economic system is an 'integral system'. In the economic realm we only deal with goods and services, and the flow of economic values. This social realm of economy stands in polarity to the realm of spirituality, which includes all aspects of human faculties and skills. Between these two we have a third, the realm of rights, and the law. In the spiritual or cultural realm each human being is treated individually. In the economic realm everything is always concerned with groups and communities joining together and collaborating. In the rights realm, we have rights that are the same for each human being, so we could say it is the 'generally human sphere' of equality. It is in this sphere that human dignity can and has to be redeemed and preserved.

When an enterprise gives money to a worker or an employee this means the worker is obliged to invest his skills in the work of this enterprise. These processes and agreements that arise from the rights life

Joseph Beuys, Das Kapital Raum (the Capital Space) 1970–1977, Schaffhausen, Switzerland

are physically manifested in money, and govern economic processes. But today the realms are mixed and the boundaries blurred. Money has no intrinsic economic value; it is drawn from the central bank system in a free and independent act. This freely drawn money is given as credit to the entrepreneur. Such short-term credit finances companies' production. In the hands of the entrepreneur the money then becomes the money of the enterprise. There it is used to give an income to all employees or co-workers, including the entrepreneur. In the hand of employees the money is transformed into the right to purchase produced goods and services in the market. The circulation of money is similar to the circulation of our blood. It is a closed system with processes of development and decomposition. So the bank system has to take care that the money that has been dispatched finally comes back to the central bank. The circulation has to come full circle again after a certain time. These briefly outlined aspects make it clear that in the modern economy, money has metamorphosed into a rights document, a token.

Wherever money gets stuck in the sphere of goods and services within the economy, this hinders healthy social processes—it obstructs and destroys.

> We need only recall the fact that money, by becoming a real object in economic transactions, deludes men as to its true nature, and by producing this imaginary effect at the same time tyrannizes over them.[1]

The third area of the social realm, the rights life, thus contains everything that is directly connected with human individuality and not with the circulation of economic values. This concerns each human being in the same way, and therefore this is the realm where human dignity can and must be restored.

One can see from unprejudiced study of the phenomena that the social organism has developed in more recent times in a threefold way: first of all we have the sphere connected with human capacities, with the expression of each individuality. The faculties of each human being are the source of spiritual and cultural life. What each particular person brings to earth by virtue of his individual destiny, can only be recognized and judged by individual consciousness. Freedom alone is the basis of this sphere.

The other sphere is the area of social initiatives. A producer offers goods or services and then a group of consumers judge the value of these. Rudolf Steiner refers to these relationships as associations. People working together create the economic values which are always oriented to the needs of other human beings. Herein the principle of fraternity realizes itself in an objective way. Between them we have a third sphere, the rights sphere. This is the sphere of agreement, obligation and entitlement. Out of the principle of freedom, we must also grant freedom to every human being. Every human being is equally entitled to freedom, and thus the social principle we must work with in this third sphere is equality.

There are three false concepts that strongly influence our economy today. The first false concept is private property in the production sphere. Here we need a new concept of ownership of enterprises, so that the entrepreneur can realize his free initiative and his creativity. To be able to do this he needs the appropriate means of production. He has to be free to do with the means of production what he feels to be right within the framework that the associations have assigned. The means of production should not be sold or inherited arbitrarily. The concept of private ownership falls away—it makes no sense in a modern economy.

The second false concept is profit as a driving force of the economy. Just because a surplus can be made in an enterprise does not give the entrepreneur the right to dictate the use of economic values. Making profit cannot be the only aim of an enterprise. We need to replace the material incentive with an incentive that arises from interest in the other, so that our incentive becomes that of meeting the needs of other human beings. This requires insight into the general context of social conditions around the world—which includes every human being on earth.

The third false concept is paid labour. This is a concept from the bartering economy of the Middle Ages. Most of the social conflicts and problems in industrial society have evolved from this false concept. The demand by Karl Marx that 'work cannot become a commodity' results from his reaction to this false concept. The modern human being feels that his integrity is diminished by selling his skills. In reality, giving an income to employees and the entrepreneur is not an economic fact but a matter of the rights life. Paying for labour is not in line with the modern economy. All employees should be given a fair and just income in accordance with the whole. So the procedure of giving an income must be transferred from the economic sphere to the rights sphere. Each human being has a right to an income that enables them to live with dignity and integrity. Only if each human being is given such an income can they share their skills and abilities with their fellow human beings.

You can see that if we transform our view of capital, tremendous change could happen in the social realm. I would like to point out again

Beuys exhibiting a photograph of Rudolf Steiner

that I am not interested in making any suggestions for *how* one could arrange the world in a better way. I have just tried to picture and describe the reality of social processes—the essence of social reality. We often handle these social processes in the modern world, but we do not always have the appropriate depth of understanding. Beuys had this understanding and deep insights. He was able to think these new concepts of capital and money, and he used this understanding to foster a movement for social renewal.

I believe that Beuys achieved a vision of threefolding and social sculpture in a way that advanced Rudolf Steiner's ideas. If a large enough number of people start to shape the world out of these new spiritual insights it will be possible to make our social conditions healthier. The aim will not be to create a new paradise but to address what is wrong in our modern society, so that the social organism can follow the laws of its intrinsic nature and develop in a healthy way. All people who collaborate in this task are partners in creating this social sculpture.

In this way, 'we are the revolution!'

Beuys's concept

Beuys's concept of money can be clearly understood in the blackboard sketches he made (see picture, over). What stands out especially on the blackboard is the circulation of money above which is written: **Kunst = Kapital (art = capital)**.

In the diagram '*Art = Capital*', one sees the money circuit in a broader context. Under this title, Beuys has drawn an arrow from art to economy; and underneath another arrow which runs counter to the first, representing mutual dependence. Above this, he clarifies by writing '*art—creativity = labour, work*'. This explains Beuys's concept of work. Work has its source in the potential of human creativity. It becomes active in enterprises where nature is transformed into a consumable commodity.

An essential point of view contained in this diagram is that the democratic central bank is depicted as the heart (middle/left). Beuys links this with a new physiological perspective that has been established in Goethean science, and sees the heart not at all as a pump but rather as a harmonizing organ. The central bank is, therefore, not to be looked upon

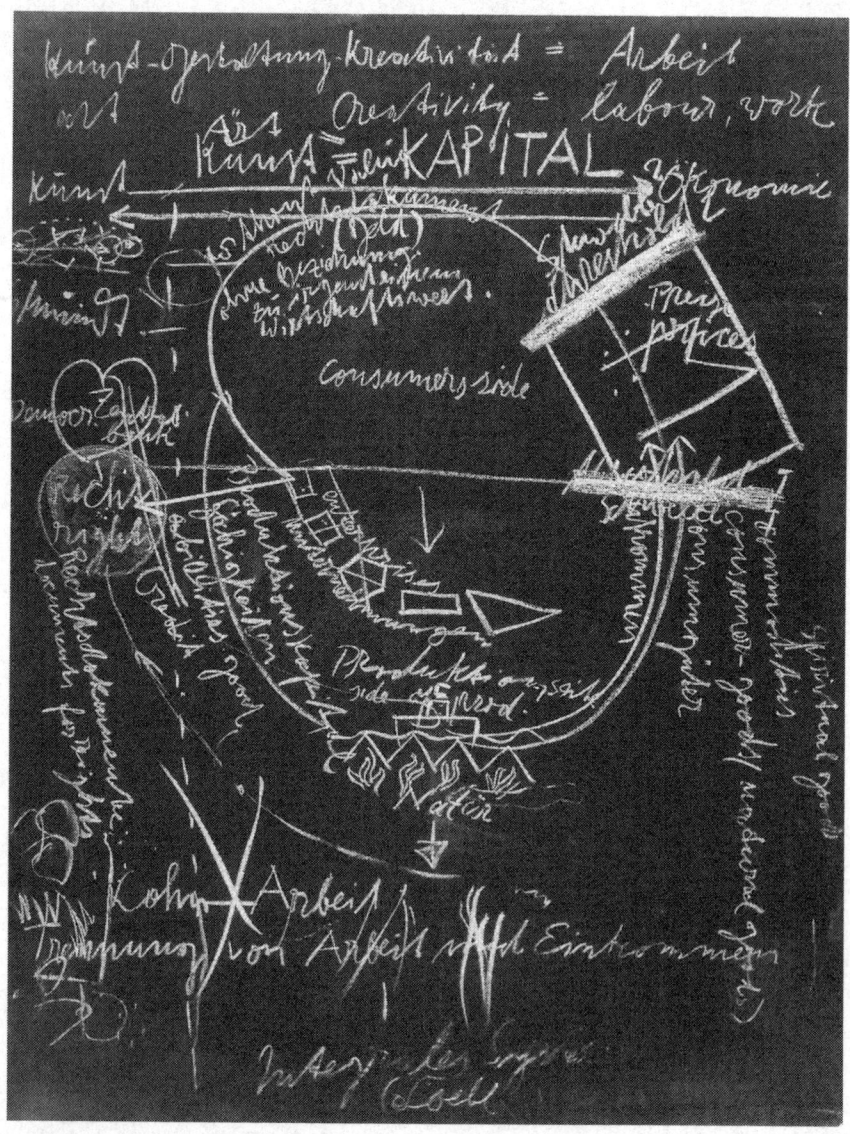

The blackboard 'Art = Capital' exhibited in Beuys's installation 'The Capital Space 1970–1977' at 'Hallen für neue Kunst' in Schaffhausen, Switzerland.

as a hierarchical organ that pumps money into the economy at its discretion, but as a regulating and harmonizing social organ.

The creation of money is determined by the initiative of people. Next to 'enterprises' ('*Unternehmungen*', on the right), Beuys writes that the '*abilities*' of people are credited. They are also called '*production capital*', as written on the blackboard.

In this picture we can see both the production and consumption sides, marked by a horizontal line. 'Documents for rights' ('*Rechtsdokumente*') is written on the left under Central Bank. Money is not an economic value any more, but instead it has become an element of the rights life. On the production side, Beuys lists the various forms of enterprises, characterized by geometric figures, and below this '*nature*' in its manifold forms. People, by working together collectively in production, transform nature through their skills into consumer goods. The expression hired labour ('*Lohn-Arbeit*') is indicated by a bold 'X'; this is the past. In today's world it is '*Separation of work and income*'. One is activity in the economic realm and the other is in the legal rights sphere.

On the right-hand side, at the bottom of the diagram, Beuys refers to the Czechoslovakian economist, Eugen Loebl, who, as we saw above, coined the term integral system ('Integrales System') for the entire modern production side.

Consumer goods manufactured by enterprises flow into the market (right/top '*Schwelle*' or threshold under capital 'M' = market). All the money paid out to enterprises within the currency domain must be taken into account when calculating the prices ('*Preise*') of the product. At the threshold of the market, all produced goods are taken out of the economic circuit and the money flows back to the enterprises. One has to now ensure that the money, '*without connection to any economic value*' (middle/top), comes back to the democratic central bank system. Above the heart of the modern money circuit, Beuys has written the name of the Goethean scientist *Wilhelm Schmundt*, whom he reveres as '*our great teacher*'.

Note

1. Rudolf Steiner: *The Social Future*, GA 332a, Anthroposophic Press, New York 1972, p. 38.

3. Just Bananas ...

The Social Organism as a Work of Art

The banana is the most important export fruit in the world. More than 11 million tons are exported every year. More than one million tons every year are shipped to Germany (more than 14 kg per head). Most bananas come from Central or Latin America, and most of them from huge plantations. There is little consideration for the human being or for the environment in the cultivation of bananas. Neglect of even the elementary dignity of man, oppression of the poor in the countryside, and the ruthless exploitation of nature still shape people's lives in the *zona bananera*.

The market is shaped by the globally powerful multinationals like Chiquita, Dole, Del Monte and Fyffes, who collectively control the cultivation, transport and commerce of this funny curved fruit. The size of the multinationals allows them to fix prices, to be ruthless with people and the environment, and to put pressure on regional and national governments to support them—or to face their wrath.

How different would our social conditions be if we the consumers saw the face of the producers behind the products? Such a very special fruit like the banana could become the starting point for a meditation. How did this fruit come into my hand? Who were the individuals involved in the distribution process? How were the bananas transported from the cultivation area to me? How did the bananas get from the cultivation and harvest areas to the port? Under what agricultural and social conditions were the bananas cultivated? Were they an organically cultivated fruit, grown with healthy cooperation between human beings and nature, or were they the result of a soulless agro-technical-chemical process that alienates and enslaves human beings, that poisons and contaminates nature? What is life like for our fellow human beings on the banana plantations these days? What are the living conditions of the farmers, whose accomplishment I now enjoy in this beautiful fruit? Can I eat this banana with a good feeling—or will I become sick if I know the reality of their cultivation? These are the numerous questions I typically cannot answer as a 'passive' consumer. Are we even faintly conscious of such intricate social connections?

Reading Shelley Sacks's book, EXCHANGE VALUES—*Images of*

Invisible Lives will, however, stimulate such questions. Not in the form of clumsy 'political art', but in a finer and deeper form. The viewer needs to become active, establish relationships, has to connect himself with the life and the fate of the producers at the other end of the economic chain. Isn't it here that the true quality of modern art can be experienced?: 'Art is the mediator of the inexpressible.' (Goethe)

Every glance at the products we use every day could actually link us with the entirety of humanity. If we were to practise this consistently we would very quickly find ourselves connected with the people who produce goods—indeed with the whole of humanity. Even the most stubborn, self-sufficient person cannot exclude himself from this link with other people, which is a global connection. Yes, it is the division of labour and global collaboration that has brought great economic and technological achievements, as well as many advancements that make life easier for modern humankind. In addition to this, worldwide data and communication networks have led to an opening up of space and time.

However, economic and political interests have drawn on these positive developments in order to increase their power. Mankind's development has thus been grasped by those who are powerful, and turned around to prevent the development of freedom. This, however, does not mean that the problem lies with a world-embracing collaboration of people, but rather that we have not yet brought sufficient awareness to bear on these modern economic developments, and have not shaped them accordingly. This could actually have led to a value-creating society oriented towards a differentiating global market that practises solidarity with others and collaboration in working towards world-encompassing wellbeing.

Joseph Beuys, the great German artist, understood this connectedness. In his lecture 'Every human being is an artist—On the way to forming the social organism into its shape of freedom', which he gave in Achberg in 1978, he clearly describes the process of economic value-formation and how money has to reflect it in an appropriate way.

Human requirements are the starting point and determiner of the goals of all economic activity. Economic values arise by transforming nature through human work, and also through intelligence that organises work—always directed at satisfying needs of the consumer. With regard to nature as well as human work, we have to develop an entirely new perception, thinking and sensitivity out of which a creative and active social formation can emerge.

Joseph Beuys, 23 March 1978 in Achberg giving his lecture: 'Every human being is an artist—On the way to forming the social organism into its shape of freedom.'

(Photo: Peter Schata)

In describing the process of economic value creation, our starting point will be human work and therewith the primal phenomenon of the socially active person. Work is always directed to the creation of a product, a service to satisfy the needs of other people. Working for the needs of others expresses a primal social gesture. While some people exist as needy beings in this world, others—who are gifted with the necessary skills or abilities—are prepared to satisfy these needs. The direction of this process changes continuously. Everyone has specific abilities that can be used to satisfy the needs of his fellow men. On the other hand, everyone also has many needs and thus has to rely on the services of other people. Abilities and needs: both are informed by each person's unique individuality.

With this we have provided a passing description of how economic values arise. Work transforms Nature so that a consumable product emerges. Human ability and intelligence organise work so it may be meaningfully and effectively employed. This basically describes the formation of value in business as well as the primal phenomenon of economic life.

The principle of universal collaboration, on the other hand, depends upon consistent care for others. This basically means that in a society that has absolutely no unemployment, no one can produce anything for himself any more. All production and all work are directed to the needs of other people. Work-providing businesses strive towards world-encompassing, fraternal collaboration.

This domain of production stands as a complement to the domain of consumption. A person's requirements can only be determined by himself—this is completely individual. The requirements of consumption arise from individual personalities.

Work, which is a producing activity, is always accompanied by other processes: an agreement is made, and a person becomes obliged to use his abilities in production. On the other hand, he receives at the same time the right to purchase a specific quantity of goods produced in correlation to his needs. In the modern **economy of abilities**, these legal processes are expressed by using money as a legal element. This economic form is thus also correctly referred to as a money economy.

These other processes are completely different from those described earlier: with entitlements and obligations we have the **primal phenomena of rights**. These legal processes are essentially mediated within economic life by money. When money moves from the company income side, as part of collective production, to become income to the individual employees, this signifies a legal act; on the one hand this obliges the employee to use his abilities at this enterprise, but once in the hands of the employee, the money signifies an entitlement to acquire a supply of produced goods. The qualitative difference can also be recognized in the fact that this legal demand can only have validity within a legal community, a nation, while economic activity today can only be thought of in a global context, of the world economy.

Thus we see how the primary processes of economic life, so to say, contain and direct legal processes, mediated through their affiliations with money. Every payment made by the consumer obliges the producer to link his abilities to a particular product. Ultimately, it is always the consumer who controls and directs economic processes through his purchase decisions.

Work is a primary human ability or capacity. The essence of work is that it is goal-oriented and meaningful. With this, another domain develops, again with a new quality. We will call this the domain where sense and meaning is experienced, involving goal-setting; a 'business-oriented intellectuality'. This intellectuality permeates all business domains with a network of management bodies. Objectives are set here, are organized, and the entire activity receives meaning. Business-orientated decision-making bodies find insight into a situation, build a foundation for making judgements, and initiate the formation of an economic organism in which everyone is active.

The social organism thus takes a threefold form. There is the intellect, which is always linked with people's individual abilities, and is part of our spiritual life; law, which regulates relationships between people and is part of our life of rights; and the economy, within which all people work in a society towards future world goals, as our economic life.

Human work cannot really be paid for; only the results of the work can be given a measurable price. Beuys wrote on the blackboard reproduced here:

'wenn nur mit diesem Kapital
bezahlt werden kann,
muß mit Menschenwürde
und Menschenrecht
bezahlt werden!'

'if this capital is the only means of
   paying,
then it must be paid
with human dignity
and human rights!'

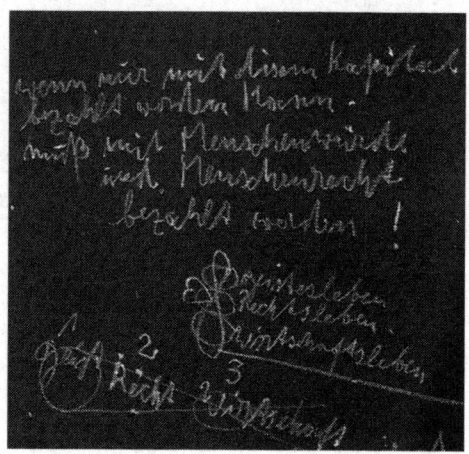

> Spiritual Life
> Rights Life
> Economic Life

The processes of a modern economic society are found in the division of labour, the production of goods to provide for the consumption of others, and the methods of collective production. No part of the earth is any longer in a position to be completely self-supporting. Only a worldwide co-operative effort can do justice to the requirements of post-industrial production methods and thereby provide the foundation for a post-materialistic world order.

The streams of economic values, whose emergence have been described above, are accompanied by legal processes, of employed people committed to co-operation, and likewise an entitlement for the consumer as regards produced goods and services. These legal processes are expressed through money. Money, as a legal element, serves to regulate these correlations. Money, like our life in the legal sphere, must be placed on a democratic foundation. Legal processes can thus be shaped into a new contract in accord with equality.

Freedom, Equality and Fraternity are the functioning principles of a modern society built on self-administration. These can only achieve the measure of a human being when they correspond to his essence in a threefold manner: freedom in his spiritual life, equality in the legal sphere, and fraternity in his economic life (Rudolf Steiner).

Only when a sufficiently large number of people having these new insights want to take charge of shaping the world, can social relationships be healed. The revival and strong growth of the worldwide movement for civil society will inevitably help this to come about. 'Créativité au Pouvoir', 'Let creativity rule,' was the slogan of the May 1968 Uprising in

Paris. This battle-cry is even more valid today. To see through and recognize social development trends and processes is one side of what is needed, while artistic and creative development of new social forms must join this. Then people of goodwill can collectively create a different, better world that is worthy of the human being.

We cannot strive to produce a paradisiacal condition, but we can eliminate the host of dysfunctions and disorders in our society so as to enable the social organism to develop in a healthy manner corresponding to its intrinsic nature. All those who work to bring this about are fellow creators and artists of the social sculpture. It is therefore with good reason that this presentation concludes with the words of one of the most significant artists of the last century:

> *Only where concepts are radically enhanced will it be possible today to introduce something, by working with art, that proves art to be the only evolutionary force capable of dismantling the repressive effect of an outmoded social system tottering in confusion towards its demise, and to build A SOCIAL ORGANISM AS A WORK OF ART ... EVERY PERSON IS AN ARTIST, who, through his own directly experienced freedom—which is the place where freedom arises—learns to shape the material that confronts him within a FUTURE SOCIAL ORDER AS A TOTAL WORK OF ART. Here self-determination and co-determination arise in the cultural domain (freedom), in legal structures (democracy) and in the economic realm (socialism)—and thus autonomy and decentralization (threefold structure): A FREE DEMOCRATIC SOCIALISM.*[1]

Only by developing radical new concepts can ART and WORK evolve a force to demonstrate that ART is the only revolutionary power, with the capacity to re-imagine an outmoded and dying social system to create a SOCIAL ORDER AS A TOTAL WORK OF ART.

In art, ultimately, the *object* is not as important as how we embody art in our interrelations. In a broader view of things, the *process* enhances what may otherwise be an apparently trivial *product*, creatively extending it into other human dimensions. Art itself becomes an act of freedom as the viewer becomes part of the work of art. Then a social sculpture emerges. Thus we come back to Shelley Sacks's 'EXCHANGE VALUES'—but also to the gift Friedrich Schiller gave us in his '*Letters on the Aesthetic Education of Man*':

> *The philosophical spirit of investigation, urgently required by the circum-*

stances of our times, involves a realization that the highest form of art is to create political freedom.

That says it all . . .

Note

1. Joseph Beuys: 'Ich durchsuche Feldcharakter' ('I search through field character'), in *Soziale Plastik*, Harlan et al, p. 121.

4. Spirituality and Social Action: Mahatma Gandhi and Rudolf Steiner

'But although high in intellectual attainments, many Westerners are caught up in rank materialism...
East and West must now establish a golden middle path, of action wedded to spirituality.'

Paramahansa Yogananda[1]

Mahatma Gandhi and Rudolf Steiner are doubtless two of the most outstanding individuals of the 20th century.[2] One originated from India—which, although situated in the west of Asia, might be called the heart of Asia—the other from German-speaking Europe, or we may say: the heart of Europe. Both united their spiritual striving with social research and social action and can be called shining exemplars for future humanity. They are surely both forerunners of modern cosmopolitanism.

Mahatma Gandhi was in many areas very successful with his fight for a free, independent India. The 'swaraj'[3] nation was born at midnight of 15 August 1947; but only a short time after this, Gandhi was assassinated—on 30 January 1948—by the Hindu fanatic Nathuram Godse. It seems that India learnt little from the Mahatma's wisdom. Bertrand Russell said: 'Independent India paid huge reverence to Gandhiji, but it ignored all his teachings.' Subsequently, Nehru's India took a completely different direction, pursuing the path of power politics.

Rudolf Steiner's social activities were at first sight not as successful as Gandhi's. But it seems as if two or three generations after Rudolf Steiner's involvement in social issues, the fruitfulness of his social ideas is at last being proved. Many social activities based on his ideas of the threefold social order are flourishing all over the world: over 2,500 schools and kindergartens, residential homes for children and adults with learning difficulties, thousands of farms working with the biodynamic method, medical institutions working with his spiritually extended approach to medicine, successful entrepreneurs inspired by Steiner's social ideas in the economic realm, and even flourishing banks, inspired by his new concepts of money and economics.

Joseph Huber, a professor of social science at Halle-Wittenberg University in Germany states: 'Whoever wishes to overcome the contemporary crisis and take part in building a human future has to go beyond Karl Marx, but he never should overlook Rudolf Steiner's ideas.'

Gandhi and Steiner—the spiritual background

In European intellectual life, Rudolf Steiner is credited with introducing a new spiritual impulse to a world that had become increasingly materialistic. In the nineteenth century, he had a very critical outlook on religion. He was also initially critical of theosophy. Yet possessed of a very individual way of thinking characterized by a penetrating search for knowledge and insights, he joined the Theosophical Society in 1902 and became the General Secretary of the recently formed German section. Steiner was able to recognize the value of the most varied esoteric and religious streams, and their culmination in Christianity. In 1913 he independently founded the Anthroposophical Society.

Steiner developed the highest regard for Indian esotericism. In his lectures on the esoteric foundations of the Bhagavad Gita, he referred to it as 'one of the most penetrating manifestations of the human spirit ... whose foundations, ancient as they are, are of renewed importance to us today.'[4]

He rejected any form of 'guru-dom'. As he saw it, modern man must replace the guru with mental training: 'By this, I don't refer to intellectual-philosophical training only but to the development of every level of awareness that exists when one practises a contemplative, inward-looking process.' Steiner also rejected submissive adherence to a teacher because he felt that everyone must find the source of awareness within himself and must examine everything using his own thinking faculties.

In his youth, Gandhi passed through an absolutely atheistic phase. Prompted by his interaction with theosophy in 1890, he began to study the Bhagavad Gita and Hinduism. Annie Besant's book *How I Became a Theosophist* strengthened his growing aversion to atheism. He then studied the Bible, in particular the New Testament, which fascinated him, and the Koran, the holy book of Islam. Moving towards Christianity was however very difficult for Gandhi since he had had very negative experiences with Christian missionaries in his youth. Nevertheless, his close inner connection to the New Testament, in particular elements of the Sermon on the Mount, stood in sharp contrast to this:

> Towards the end of my second year in England I came across two theosophists, brothers, and both unmarried. They talked to me

about the Gita. They were reading Sir Edwin Arnold's translation—*The Song Celestial*—and they invited me to read the original with them. I felt ashamed, as I had read the divine poem neither in Sanskrit nor in Gujarati. I was obliged to tell them that I had not read the Gita, but that I would gladly read it with them, and that though my knowledge of Sanskrit was meagre, still I hoped to be able to understand the original to the extent of telling where the translation failed to bring out the meaning. I began reading the Gita with them ... The book struck me as one of priceless worth. The impression has ever since been growing on me with the result that I regard it today as the book *par excellence* for the knowledge of Truth ...

But the New Testament produced a different impression, especially the Sermon on the Mount which went straight to my heart. I compared it with the Gita. The verses, 'But I say unto you, that you resist not evil: but whosoever shall smite thee on thy right cheek, turn to him the other also. And if any man take away thy coat let him have thy cloak too', delighted me beyond measure ... My young mind tried to unify the teaching of the Gita, the *Light of Asia* and the Sermon on the Mount. That renunciation was the highest form of religion appealed to me greatly ... To see the universal and all-pervading Spirit of Truth face to face one must be able to love the meanest of creation as oneself. And a man who aspires after that cannot afford to keep out of any field of life. That is why my devotion to Truth has drawn me into the field of politics; and I can say without the slightest hesitation, and yet in all humility, that those who say that religion has nothing to do with politics do not know what religion means ...

In bidding farewell to the reader, for the time being at any rate, I ask him to join with me in prayer to the God of Truth that He may grant me the boon of *Ahimsa* in mind, word and deed.[5]

As regards potential followers, he said:

Truth and Ahimsa will never perish; however, if Gandhi-ism is just another name for sectarianism, then it has earned its demise ... Nobody should call himself a follower of Gandhi. It will suffice that I am my own follower ... That in itself is already an exacting path.[6]

Despite his religious background, Gandhi was committed not only to free will in general but in particular to responsible creation of the future through acts of free will by individuals. He was also convinced that any individual would be able to act according to his free will only if he was economically independent.

Initially Gandhi focused on the power one has over oneself and not on the creation of new types of power over others. His understanding of autonomy also encompassed the meaning of self-catharsis and self-actualization. Self-catharsis (brahmacharya) can be subdivided into three components: fearlessness, independence (depending on oneself) and self-identification. Gandhi had a deep understanding of dharma and karma. 'To find the truth means to find yourself, to find your own destiny, in other words: to become perfect.'

Both Gandhi and Steiner regarded education as the continual shaping of future generations who form the foundation of social healing. This, however, requires both schools and culture that are allowed to unfold without any interference from politics and economics. Gandhi was in favour of conversion and not force; he provided germinal motivation about how a modern school can be structured. With his Waldorf Schools, Steiner provided a comprehensive concept for an education intended for all people— beyond social classes, and beyond all selection by race, nation or intellect—where children of all kinds can be educated in a truly human and cosmopolitan way.

The social approach

Rudolf Steiner developed a view of society through his approach to philosophy, founded on our intrinsic capacity for freedom, and in this manner arrived at the following fundamental sociological law. In the early stages of cultural evolution, he said, humanity tends towards the formation of social units where initially the interests of individuals are sacrificed to the interests of these associations. The further course of development leads to the emancipation of the individual from the interests of the association, and to unrestricted development of the needs and capacities of the individual.[7]

Rudolf Steiner recognizes social reality as an organic phenomenon. His phenomenological studies enabled him to recognize the inner laws and structures of social phenomena. He thus contributed to overcoming the limitations of all existing social ideologies.

Steiner describes the task for both economists and social scientists thus: insightful thinking can understand phenomena appearing in the world such that their underlying concept can become manifest; in other words, phenomena appear in their purest form during our thinking process. Steiner describes this path in all his lectures as well as in his course on

World Economy.⁸ Having described phenomena in the world, we can allow their causes, laws, or essence to emerge in our thinking by exercising our own will.

We are polarized between the aspect of the past (engaging as we do with a formed and 'finished' world) and the present (in a free act, we initiate actions and reconfigure the world). These two elements can be merged in social art: existing social relationships, human relationships and organizations are the substance with which the artist can work, and whose properties he must clearly understand. The 'beautiful' social form (Friedrich Schiller) is a human artistic creation. Social capabilities that we have acquired correspond to the artist's command of his craft. The idea towards which we are working springs from social laws. This, however, requires artistic intuition for doing the right thing at the right time together with other people.

'Gandhi was a saint who worked as a lawyer.'⁹ Uniquely, he had the capacity to combine the lawyer, the politician and saintliness in one person. For Gandhi too, 'individuality is the actual source of all progress'. He developed his social ideas from his own experiences in non-violent political conflict:

> Satyagraha is not physical force. A satyagrahi does not inflict pain on the adversary; he does not seek his destruction ... Satyagraha is pure soul-force. Truth is the very substance of the soul. That is why this force is called satyagraha. The soul is informed with knowledge. In it burns the flame of love. If someone gives us pain through ignorance, we shall win him through love.¹⁰

The social and political concept

Steiner developed his idea of the threefold social order as the shape of the social organism through his experience of a century of modern industrial society in the form of liberal capitalism.

Interestingly, it was in the course of his observation of basic social forms that Steiner perceived that our now asocial modern society had, hidden within itself, the seed of true 'socialism' and of encompassing fraternal co-existence. In fact, industrial society demands selfless activity of people on behalf of one another. Liberalistic ideology, which talks of egotism in all our social relationships, is opposed to this—and this informs and impacts on our contemporary society:

> In a community of human beings working together, the well-being of the community will be the greater, the less the individual claims

> for himself the proceeds of work he has himself done; i.e. the more of these proceeds he gives over to his fellow workers, and the more his own requirements are satisfied, not out of his work, but out of work done by the others ... Every institution in a community of human beings that acts contrary to this law will inevitably engender in some part of it, after a while, suffering and want. It is a fundamental law which holds good for all social life with the same absoluteness and necessity as any law of nature within a particular field of natural causation. It must not be supposed, however, that it is sufficient to acknowledge this law as one for general moral conduct, or to try and interpret it as a general sentiment that everyone should work for the good of his fellow man. No, this law only finds its living, fitting expression in actual reality, when a community of human beings succeeds in creating institutions of such a kind that no one can ever claim the results of his own labour for himself, but where they all, to the last fraction, go wholly to the benefit of the community. And he, again, must himself be supported in return by the labours of his fellow human beings. The important point is, therefore, that working for one's fellow man, and the object of obtaining a certain income, must be kept apart, as two separate things.[11]

In pointing to this fundamental social law, Rudolf Steiner quotes the great Buddha: 'Hate is not overcome by hate, but by love alone'; and he concludes, 'We touch here upon something, the recognition of which can alone lead to any real "social thinking".'

Twelve years after that fundamental social law, Steiner discovered the phenomenon of the threefold organism in the human being and in the social realm:

> The social organism is structured like a biological organism. And just as thinking occurs via the head and not through the lungs, so the social organism needs to be divided into separate systems, each of which has its own specific function and autonomy yet also works together harmoniously with the others. Economic life can only thrive if it develops as an autonomous 'limb' of the social organism, according to its own forces and laws. It is thrown into confusion when another limb of the social organism, the political state, takes it over and controls it. The political limb should instead remain quite separate and independent alongside the economy, just as the respiratory system works separately from, but in harmony with the

head. Their harmonious cooperation cannot be achieved through a single legislative and administrative 'organ' that controls both systems, but by the separate legislative and administrative bodies of each system creating a living interaction with one another. The political sphere can do no other than destroy economic life when it takes control of it; and the economic sphere loses its strength and vitality when it tries to become political.[12]

Gandhi's background was the rural society based on village agriculture, from which he developed a decentralized social structure built on small, independent units. Sarvodaya, as Gandhi understood it, is based on villages, and is anti-urban:

> Centralization as a system is not to be merged with a non-violent social structure. The centre of power is now in New Delhi or in Calcutta and Bombay, in the big cities. I would rather that it was distributed over the seven thousand villages of India.[13]

Power, he believed, should be moved from the centre to smaller, social units and all members living in this unit should participate in decision processes. Gandhi was very sceptical about parliamentary democracy and worked towards a more direct form of democracy. Apart from direct democracy, Gandhi was also in favour of building a type of democratic consensus that in turn called for manageable social units:

> Ahimsa, the law of love. Brotherhood is now only a distant aspiration. To me it is a test of true spirituality. All our prayers, fasting and observances are empty nothings so long as we do not feel a live kinship with all life. But we have not even arrived at that intellectual belief, let alone a heart realization. We are still selective. A selective brotherhood is a selfish partnership. Brotherhood requires no consideration or response.[14]

The economic concept

> One could at most compare individual countries to cells of an organism; as an economic body, the entire world can only be compared to an organism. We have to note this. Ever since we have had a world economy, it has been much easier to understand that individual countries can only be compared to cells. The whole earth considered as an economic organism, is (actually) the social organism...[15]

Steiner had already developed the concept of a globalized economy in the 1920s. His concept, however, was oriented to the intrinsic nature of the human being. The key to fraternal collaboration lies in the division of labour among people. Every person who is economically active produces something for the requirement of others. Others ensure that he can create a humane existence for himself; they generate food, clothing, housing etc. for him. This is solidarity in give and take.

This results in a totally new approach to economic processes. Steiner's concept of an industrial society and a post-industrial economy attempts to unite free people who have initiative with this principle of economic solidarity. To this end, he explains the form of an associative economic life in which fraternal elements and free initiative are brought together in an original form. The main problem, as Steiner saw it, was the sundering of production and consumption interests (producers' and consumers' interests).

A new social form is required to bridge this polarity. The market mechanism always functions in hindsight and is extremely vulnerable to any manipulation. In the place of an abstract, mechanistic market, Rudolf Steiner developed a picture of an organic, associative economy built on human relationships. Opposing groups acting in the economic field should have 'round table' discussions to discover their divergent interests and balance each other. This association would result in 'automatic rationality and objective public spirit' (Steiner).

Associative economy creates a new form of freedom whereby regional associations of this kind ensure that consumers' interests are fully represented alongside those of producers. Collaboration between independent institutions, both economic and cultural, and dialogue between economic *and* cultural institutions, each with their equal say, would enable any surpluses to benefit cultural institutions directly, rather than via State subsidies—a more complex and costly route. Such associations should be attached to bank-type institutions entrusted with implementing association decisions. The credit provided by these banks should also be subject to the association's decisions. Rudolf Steiner viewed the founding of such 'associative banks' as vital.

Self-governing village communities are the starting point for Gandhi's economic approach. Self-reliance was to be created here, placing inhabitants in the position of being able to provide for themselves. The beginnings of his Khadi movement sprang from this. Gandhi was convinced that private ownership of the means of production would lead to a system of material exploitation as well as spiritual alienation. He came up with a new form of ownership in which an administrator would function as a trustee of the people—who could withdraw their mandate at any time:

> Working for economic equality means abolishing the eternal conflict between capital and labour. It means the levelling down of the few rich in whose hands is concentrated the bulk of the nation's wealth on the one hand, and the levelling up of the semi-starved naked millions on the other. A non-violent system of government is clearly an impossibility so long as the wide gulf between the rich and the hungry millions persist ... I adhere to my doctrine of trusteeship in spite of the ridicule that has been poured upon it. It is true that it is difficult to reach. So is non-violence...[16]

> Non-possession is allied to non-stealing. A thing not originally stolen must nevertheless be classified as stolen property, if we possess it without needing it. Possession implies provision for the future. A seeker after truth, a follower of the law of Love cannot hold anything against tomorrow. God never stores for the morrow; he never creates more than what is strictly needed for the moment. If therefore we repose faith in His providence, we should rest assured, that He will give us every day our daily bread, meaning everything that we require. Saints and devotees, who have lived in such faith, have always derived a justification for it from their experience...[17]

Since Gandhi always experimented with truth, continually re-orienting it to reality, his suggestions always lent themselves to perennial renewal. I am convinced that Gandhi would have been able to provide a completely new economic concept for the 21st century, in complete alignment with his basic principles.

> Where Gandhi's direction was local and very green, Steiner developed a path that was fully compatible with Gandhi's spirit and simultaneously led the way towards a reality that Gandhi had to attend to. Gandhi's reality was India of the mid-twentieth century—this enormous, spread-out collection of villages with a couple of far-flung metropolises of rather exploitational character.[18]

The political strategy

At the end of the First World War, Steiner was in touch with the highest-ranking government functionaries. Prince Max von Baden, the last Chancellor of the German Reich, was as familiar with the concept of the threefold order as the last Austrian Emperor, Karl. The heads of government did not, however, have the inclination or the military support to convert these ideas into reality. A short while later, therefore, Steiner presented a broad educational programme directly to the public, envisaging the possibility of precipitating this new social order mainly through the awareness and pressure of a sufficiently large number of people.

> Actually, we cannot even discuss current demands, since they are historical demands. Socialism is a historical demand, and we can properly understand it only in that sense. Democracy is a historical demand. However, liberalism, freedom, individualism are also historical demands, but modern people seldom notice them as such. It is not possible to discuss the situation further unless we recognize the social organism in its three aspects: socialism in economic life, democracy in the life of rights, and freedom or individuality in cultural life.
>
> That is in truth the only salvation for humanity. Although those are the intense and unyielding historical trends of the present, we should not delude ourselves into thinking that no other demands will appear for those who have deep insight into the situation. Adults need to live in a society that is economically social, governmentally democratic, and culturally free.[19]

Apart from his work in the educational field, Steiner also recognized the significance and necessity of a practical, social model. This led to the founding of the Free Waldorf School in Stuttgart. Economic enterprises, agricultural operations, cultural and health institutions would be integrated in an economic association for the purpose of collaborating in the development of a new kind of fraternity.

The year 1920 saw the formation of such an associative entity in Stuttgart. This was 'The Coming Day', a public limited company for promoting economic and spiritual values. A short while later saw the founding of 'Futurum AG' (a 'public limited company') in Dornach. On the one hand people who saw these undertakings as valid and meaningful, deposited money in them. On the other, an entire range of existing businesses was integrated into them. Entrepreneurs gave up their control over the regulation of their capital but could instead run the business in a completely independent manner. Capital was only charged at a 5 per cent interest rate and the entrepreneur received a fixed income. With this, an early form of neutralization of capital as had been envisioned by Steiner was achieved.

Members of the supervisory body held this position on an honorary basis, with Rudolf Steiner assuming chairmanship. The nature of threefold ideas meant that no kind of profit-sharing was envisaged either between the entrepreneurs or the workers. To this end, many companies organized lectures on business and other subjects, and offered eurythmy and in-service developmental courses. Business processes and relations within the enterprise were to be transparent to every employee.

Development in Germany at that time meant that it was not possible to link up with such endeavours for a long time. Only in the 1960s were there renewed efforts to rekindle the association impetus created by Rudolf Steiner. This resulted in the formation of institutions resembling banks in Bochum, Germany or the Netherlands as well as the most varied business undertakings such as the network of free enterprise initiatives in Stuttgart, Germany and the Coopera in Bern, Switzerland.

Perhaps the time is ripe to reactivate such impulses again. I do not think it is a coincidence that, in December 2005, the alternative Nobel Prize was awarded both to Nicanor Perlas for his social threefolding campaign in the Philippines, and to Ibrahim Abouleish in Egypt for his attempts to create an 'Economy Based on Love', as it was called in the laudation for the SEKEM Project. There too an attempt is being made to build association-type structures in research institutes, schools, academies and universities, various production sites, pharmaceuticals, cosmetic companies, textile production and biodynamic agriculture.

Gandhi's strategy can be best understood by his Salt March. There, he intentionally broke a senseless law, but prior to doing so, made his intentions clear to the public. His relationship with the media was ingenious. By the time he approached Dandi, the destination of his march, a huge number of people had joined it to take a direct part in this act of civil disobedience. However, the march also included or elicited the awareness of people the world over who had been informed of it through the media.

Gandhi too was always ready to talk to those in government. He always conducted his interactions with them in a manner that appealed to their nobler side. If they, however, were not ready to give him any leeway or to accept his legitimate demands, Gandhi would resort to non-violent action.

At the time of his return to India from South Africa, the Governor of Bombay wanted to speak to Gandhi. Gandhi visited His Excellency who had the following to say to him after the initial exchange of pleasantries:

'I ask one thing of you. I would like you to come and see me whenever you propose to take any steps concerning government.' I replied: 'I can very easily give the promise, inasmuch as it is my rule, as a satyagrahi to understand the viewpoint of the party I propose to deal with, and to try to agree with him as far as may be possible. I strictly observed the rule in South Africa and I mean to do the same here.'[20]

Conclusion

At a time of continual attacks and constraints on individuality, Gandhi stands as a fighter for the rebirth of the individual. This is borne by a transpersonal feeling and idea that is larger than, but encompasses all of us—the idea of humanity that Gandhi so often propounded. This humanity follows no church or denomination. The new religiosity is actually trans-religious, uniting elements of western and eastern thinking and individualizing them. This new religiosity searches for the deeper phenomenon underlying immediate sensory perceptions. Modern man wants to follow his own religious inclination and connect it with others in meditation and dialogue.

Otto Wolff, who was of German origin but lived for a very long time in India, gave a fine summary of the Mahatma's outlook:

> Gandhi believes that only the mature, the transformed, the noble, in his words, the 'spiritual' man can be a good politician, that is to say, a practical leader of men. Technical knowledge and education are nothing but prerequisites. He believes that, when man gains spirituality, the whole world gains with him, and when a man falls, the whole world falls in corresponding measure. There are so many examples of the latter and so few true examples of the former. Is not Gandhi one of these, the erring pilgrim to the eternal city as he calls himself? In our modern world we never cease to be astonished at discoveries in the field of violence. It may be that far more amazing discoveries, discoveries hitherto undreamed of, can be made—in the field of non-violence. With this message Gandhi takes leave of us.[21]

Rudolf Steiner said of Mahatma Gandhi that he might be able to introduce core Christian principles into India. By this, he naturally did not mean Christianity of the ecclesiastical variety, but the esoteric kind, a new power of love that could permeate all earthly beings. Clearly the Mahatma practised the new religion of love.

For his part, Gandhi once visited an English anthroposophical curative educational institute under the supervision of Ita Wegman, and was appreciative of the work done there. The co-workers did not have to explain anything to him. He seemed to understand with his heart the principles of their work, based on love of one's fellow man. Unfortunately, Gandhi was not able to take up Ita Wegman's invitation to visit the Goetheanum in Dornach.

Society in the West has increasingly begun to develop along the lines of self-determination, decentralization, small units, a solidarity-based economy, and individual forms of understanding, without necessarily listening to 'experts'. Gandhi advocated all these aspects. His message, in this sense, is very modern. The fact that Gandhi's real impulse has been almost forgotten in his own country does not detract from this. His impulse has future potential across the globe, thus naturally also in the West.

This applies in a similar manner to Steiner. We find more and more institutions arising throughout the world that are born from and inspired by his thinking. It is not always easy to understand his thinking and it is very difficult to pursue the path proposed by him. Daily practice, however, reveals the fruitfulness of his philosophy. Instead of closing with my own appreciation of Steiner, I would like to end with insightful words by the prominent French journalist, Jules Sauerwein, one of the most famous journalists in his time:

> I have got to know almost all monarchs of the earth, almost all prime ministers and presidents. But none of these people have left so lasting an impression on me as the Austrian philosopher and esotericist Rudolf Steiner. He was the most interesting man that I have met in my life ... Statesmen—even if they were still so powerful—always left me with the impression that they were like actors not very sure of their roles. But what a pleasure to speak with Steiner on politics! And only such an immense and rich mind is capable of understanding specific problems so precisely.

Europe and the whole world are on the way to becoming cosmopolitan. National constitutions seem overwhelmed. Consequently the modern world needs the cosmopolitan view of social and political realities. This means accepting the differences yet equal entitlement of others. It also means abolishing discrepancies between citizen rights and human rights, between natives and foreigners. In the difference we shall find the solution. The cosmopolitan view recognizes otherness. Differences are accepted and not denigrated. Difference is no longer the problem, but becomes the source of solutions. In this sense the principle of cosmopolitanism helps create social conditions that allow difference without fear.

Such an outlook turns the logic of national politics upside down: it is not national sovereignty that makes co-operation with others possible, but rather transnational co-operation that facilitates national sovereignty (Ulrich Beck).

Postscript: The future potential of Steiner and Gandhi

For many years, inspired by Steiner, people all round the world have been working on social problems without the constraints of ideological prejudice. Their concern has been to observe the phenomena of the world without judging, and they have discovered that solutions for the world's problems can be found simply by examining these phenomena with an open mind. Underlying the social order they find an image of the human being that is not just of physical but also spiritual dimensions. At the same time this is also the dimension of modern cosmopolitanism.

Steiner developed a new threefold conception of society based on this image of the human being as early as 1919. Numerous practical initiatives also arose from this new view of human nature: schools, other pedagogical institutions, initiatives for curative education and social therapy, medical and therapeutic initiatives, medicine production, biodynamic agriculture and a new approach to the arts. During the first years, these initiatives pioneered by Steiner were mainly developed in Central Europe. But thereafter many such fruitful initiatives arose, and the institutions built on these can now be found all over the world.

These successfully tested new ideas have aroused strong interest within the civil society movement. There are a number of successful projects in India founded on an understanding of the human potential that Steiner and Gandhi both articulated. In the sphere of education, there are several schools such as the Sloka School in Hyderabad. In curative education, there is the Dr. Rudolf Steiner Institute for people with learning difficulties in Dharwad, the Sadhana Village near Pune, and Friends of Camphill India in Bangalore. In biodynamic farming, there is the Maikaal project in Maheshwar involving more than 2,000 farmers, Kurinji farm in Betalgundu and Kodaikanal, the Makaibari Tea Estates in Darjeeling, and many more initiatives. And a new School of biodynamic agriculture has been established in Vinobajipuram/Tamil Nadu.

A new impulse has evolved in India: that of integrating the international potential of social threefolding ideas with practical initiatives that have already arisen there. By viewing local initiatives in India from the perspective of the worldwide threefold movement, concepts, visions and achievements can be shared and developed, and difficulties can be addressed.

To elaborate this path of inner experience, we have to free ourselves from all the ideological prejudices we are prone to as modern human beings. A path of 'meditation' or contemplation and development of our latent spiritual potential, such as I describe, may help us understand and solve the huge social problems which humanity faces today.

To do so, we have to combine deep inner spirituality with the utmost public and social engagement. If we can do this with dedication and perseverance, the veil of ignorance and our sense of impotence will slowly but surely fade. And with opened eyes we shall, step by step, be able to discover new solutions to our social predicament.

Alongside this individual path of responsibility, we will have to combine our efforts with those of many other people. This needs to be done in a deeply felt, artistic way, reaching into the depths of our creativity to persuade our fellow human beings to join our efforts to create 'a different, better world'. It requires great alertess and energy. We are all distinct individuals, and thus need to accept that there are many different ways of achieving this aim. Only then shall we have the power to achieve our collective goal: a new social sculpture. Both Gandhi and Steiner prepared the way for this.

Steiner and Gandhi: biographical details

Rudolf Steiner

1861 Born 27 February in Kraljevec, Hungary, modern Croatia.
1879 Studies mathematics, physics, natural history, philosophy and literature at Vienna's technical academy.
1882 Editor of Goethe's scientific works for Kuerschner's 'Deutscher National-literatur'.
1886 Publishes a thesis on *The Theory of Knowledge Implicit in Goethe's World Conception*.
1888 Social motto: 'Consider only true what our own thinking propels us to embrace, be active only in those social and political forms which we have ourselves given rise to; this is the important principle of the times.'
1890 Collaborative work in the Goethe-Schiller Archive at Weimar.
1891 Award of doctorate in philosophy at Rostock for his 'Theory of Knowledge'.
1893 *The Philosophy of Freedom—A Philosophy of Spiritual Activity.*
1898 Formulation of the 'fundamental sociological law'.
1899 Start of teaching activity at the school for workers' education in Berlin.
1900 Lectures at the Theosophical Library in Berlin.
1902 General Secretary of the German division of the Theosophical Society (Adyar). Development of the foundation of the future 'anthroposophy' in the following years, in volumes including: *Christianity as Mystical Fact, Theosophy, An Outline of Occult Science, Knowledge of the Higher Worlds.*
1905 Elaborates on the nature of individual self-discipline and its importance for the inner development of higher organs in *Anthroposophy and the Social Question*; formulates 'The Fundamental Social Law'. Withdraws these essays as a result of lack of interest amongst readers.
1910 Development of artistic activities: Mystery plays, stage art, eurythmy, sculpture, drawing, architecture (construction of the first Goetheanum) etc.
1913 Lectures on *The Esoteric Foundations of the Bhagavad Gita*.
'Knowledgeable people have called the sublime Bhagavad Gita the most significant philosophical poem of all mankind. And

whoever immerses himself in this awe-inspiring Gita will find this saying to be true.'
1917 Develops concepts of the threefold structure of the human and social organism.
1919 Spread of the movement for a threefold social order in southern Germany, involving discussions with working people in all large commercial establishments in the Württemberg area. Wide acceptance by the labour force and advisory bodies. Establishment of the Waldorf School; and of the enterprise 'The Coming Day', a public limited company seeking to promote economic and spiritual values. Founding of care homes for people with learning difficulties, aiming to give them a dignified way of life, bio-dynamic agriculture, The Christian Community, medical institutes etc.
1923 Founding of the General Anthroposophical Society at the Goetheanum.
1925 Died on 30 March, at Dornach.

Mahatma Gandhi

1869 Born on 2 October in Porbandar, Gujarat.
1888 Studies Law in London. Contact with the Theosophical Society. He meets Annie Besant and H. P. Blavatsky. He reads the Bhagavad Gita, the Bible and the Koran.
1891 Returns to India. Practises as a lawyer in Bombay and Rajkot.
1893 Sent to South Africa as a barrister. Gandhi becomes a political leader of the Indian immigrant community.
1904 Phoenix experimental township near Durban.
1906 Gandhi develops non-violence as a method to fight discriminatory legislation by the South African government by organising passive resistance. Sentenced to several prison terms. Satyagraha (Adherence to Truth): The inner concept of Satyagraha appears outwardly as passive resistance. At the core, however, it is much more; (it is) nothing negative, but instead positive to the highest degree imaginable. One develops an unconquerable strength when one unites oneself with the eternal satyam, with the immortal divinity. One can then single-handedly stand up to the entire world, can take upon oneself renunciation and suffering. The spiritual strength of Satyagraha which streams out from oneself, conquers the opponent without the use of physical force, through ahimsa.

1909 'Hind Swaraj' (self-rule for India). Correspondence with Tolstoy until the latter's death (20.11.1910). Tolstoy's agricultural experiments with an ideal Communist society.

1915 Returns to India. Rabindranath Tagore addresses him as 'Mahatma'. Setting up of Sabarmati Ashram in Ahmedabad.

1917 First Satyagraha action in India: for the indigo planters in Champaran, Bihar.

1919 General strike against the Rowlatt Bill which empowered the government to incarcerate people without trial. Bloodbath at Amritsar.

1920 Gandhi is elected President of the Congress. He begins his non-violent fight against the British rulers.

1921 Strike in Bardoli, Gujarat. Assault on the Police at Chauri Chaura. Gandhi breaks up the mass movement and fasts. He is sentenced to 6 years' imprisonment at Ahmedabad on grounds of incitement.

1925 Gandhi begins to write his autobiography which appears weekly. 'Individuality is the true source of all progress.'

1928 *An Autobiography. The Story of My Experiments with the Truth* and *Satyagraha in South Africa* are published.

1930 Salt March from Ahmedabad to Dandi. Gandhi is arrested and imprisoned until January 1931.

1931 Travels to London. Second Round Table Conference with no result.

1932 Campaign for the Untouchables (Harijans = Children of God).

1939 Outbreak of the Second World War. Gandhi writes to Hitler.

1942 Gandhi demands the complete independence of India: 'Quit India' resolution. He is arrested. A mass uprising takes place. Kasturba, his wife, dies in prison in Pune.

1946 Simla Conference: No agreement between Hindus and Muslims. Muslim leader, Jinnah, demands the partition of India. Gandhi calls the partition a spiritual tragedy. Bloody unrests break out in Calcutta, Bengal and Bihar and spread quickly.

1947 Partition of India and Pakistan on 15 August. 'Freedom at Midnight'.
Bomb attack on Gandhi in New Delhi. Assassinated on 30 January in New Delhi by Hindu fanatic, Nathuram Godse.

Notes

1. Paramahansa Yogananda, *Autobiography of a Yogi*, Second Indian Edition, 1975, Jaico Publishing House, Bombay.

2. Please see their biographical details at the end of this essay.
3. Swaraj means 'freedom and independence' (or self-rule/self-government).
4. Rudolf Steiner on the Bhagavad Gita, lecture of 28.5.1913 (GA 146).
5. M. K. Gandhi, *An Autobiography or the Story of my Experiments with the Truth*, p. 420, Ahmedabad 1927 and 1989.
6. M. K. Gandhi, *Young India*, 7.5.1931.
7. Rudolf Steiner, *Gesammelte Aufsätze zur Kultur- und Zeitgeschichte 1887–1901*, GA 31.
8. Rudolf Steiner, *World Economy*, GA 340, Rudolf Steiner Press, 1996.
9. Johan Galtung, *Der Weg ist das Ziel—Gandhi und die Alternativbewegung*, Wuppertal 1967.
10. Mahatma Gandhi, *Satyagraha—Not Passive Resistance, Selected works* VI.
11. Rudolf Steiner, *Anthroposophy and the Social Question*, GA 34, Mercury Press 1996.
12. Rudolf Steiner, *An Appeal to the German people and the Civilized World*, GA 24, Rudolf Steiner Press 1999.
13. Mahatma Gandhi, *Selected Works*, VI.
14. Letter from the Mahatma, 4 August 1932.
15. Rudolf Steiner, *World Economy*, GA 340, Rudolf Steiner Press, 1996, lecture of 24.7.1922.
16. Mahatma Gandhi, *Selected Works*, IV, p. 359.
17. Mahatma Gandhi, *Selected Works*, IV, p. 229.
18. Johann Galtung, *Der Weg ist das Ziel*, op. cit., p. 53.
19. Rudolf Steiner, *Education as a Force for Social Change*, GA 296, Hudson 1997, p. 10.
20. M. K. Gandhi, *An Autobiography*, op. cit., p. 312.
21. Otto Wolff, 'Gandhi's Legacy', in: *Mahatma Gandhi—as Germans See Him*, Shakuntala Publishing House (ed. Heimo Rau, Bombay and Tübingen 1976). (Heimo Rau. one of the outstanding German Indologists, professor at the University of Heidelberg, also wrote a biography of Gandhi in German, Reinbek 1970.)

5. 'We Create Social Conditions'

The Contemporary Relevance of Rudolf Steiner's Social Concepts

Just a short time after completing his first work, *The Theory of Knowledge Implicit in Goethe's World Conception* (1886), Rudolf Steiner formulated the following social maxim for contemporary society in the *Deutsche Wochenschrift* (1888):

> Consider only true what our own thinking propels us to embrace; be active only in those social and political forms which we have ourselves given rise to: this is the important principle of the times.

And following this, Rudolf Steiner elaborated insights governing a form of social science, and likewise a modern social order, which embrace humankind's essential freedom and, at the same time, challenge widespread pseudo-liberalism.

Rudolf Steiner's sociological law

After Rudolf Steiner concluded his research on Goethe, with which he was engaged throughout the latter part of the 19th century, authoring seminal works on his, Steiner's, theory of knowledge, as well as writing on philosophy, philology, culture and history, he then developed his 'fundamental sociological law'. In the work which embodies this, he suggests that one must observe all social phenomena in relation to humanity's development toward inner freedom. He named this law, which depicts the developmental movement from the collective to individuality, as the 'law of individualism'.

In the past, humanity sought to establish social collectives: everything of a personal nature was sacrificed to the interests of the community. In modern times, the individual frees himself from all constraints in order to achieve a fully free unfolding of his individuality. Today, a healthy community strives for balance between the needs of the community and the individual's development.

Workers' education

At the turn of the 20th century, Rudolf Steiner became a teacher at the Workers' Educational Institute founded by Wilhelm Liebknecht in

Berlin. His mode of teaching, and especially his creative lecturing style, appealed greatly to the workers.

It was a tragedy in Rudolf Steiner's life that he met with such great interest from a proletarian audience, but was hindered in his further activity at this school by the socialist and dogmatic director of the institute, at heart a member of the comfortable middle classes. On 15 January 1905, he gave his last lecture there. Subsequently he increased his activity in theosophical circles—where his account of spiritual experiences elicited interest; but amongst this largely bourgeois audience he did not meet with any understanding for urgent social concerns.

General Secretary of the Theosophical Society

In 1902, Rudolf Steiner became the General Secretary of the newly founded German Section of the Theosophical Society. Marie von Sivers, who later became his wife, was his close working partner.

In a magazine he published between 1903–1908, *Lucifer-Gnosis*, primarily read by members and friends of the Theosophical Society in Germany, Rudolf Steiner wrote articles in which he established the basic principles of a modern spiritual science.

In the same publication, he then described a path of schooling for the modern, Central European individual. These articles were the basis for his important, and most widely read book: *Knowledge of the Higher Worlds. How Is It Achieved?* This book ends by stating the following:

> No one, therefore, should expect the occultists of the white path to give him instruction for the development of his own egotistical self. They have not the slightest interest in the bliss of the individual. Everyone can attain that for himself, and it is not the task of the white occultists to accelerate that achievement. They are concerned entirely with the development and liberation of all beings—human beings and their fellow creatures.[1]

Theosophy and the social question—setting the stage

Articles on 'Theosophy and the Social Question' appeared in *Lucifer-Gnosis* immediately after this work (October 1905 to August 1906). Rudolf Steiner begins this series of articles with the sentence: 'Anyone at present who observes the world around us with open eyes, sees powerful signs everywhere of what one calls "the social question".'[2] The social question stands before us, he says, more palpably than at any previous time in humanity's development. This is connected with the fundamental law presented above. The human being awakens to freedom: our capacity to unfold the social qualities needed for this self-determining freedom does not initially keep pace with the development of our distinct individuality.

He carefully, almost lovingly, leads his readers to the social question:

> ... such a mode of comprehension, devoted to the highest human ideals, must gain some relationship to social needs and circumstances...
>
> [And then one seeks the fruits of this in one's feeling of satisfaction...]
>
> However, the true fruit of spiritual science may not be sought there. This fruit first shows itself when what is experienced inwardly through spiritual science is brought to bear on the tasks of practical life.[3]

The steps taken on the path of knowledge are not to be misused for personal emotional satisfaction or for the pursuit of egotistical aims. All progress on this path should be placed, fraternally, at the service of our fellow human beings.

> The real fruit of this modern path of schooling will show itself when the student of this path perceives reality in a more differentiated and exact manner, and also becomes ever more awake, with more presence of mind for the solving of the great problems of our time, especially the social question. Modern spiritual knowledge does not withdraw from life, but instead makes mastery of the problems and tasks of the outer world more practicable, in a form corresponding to spiritual and human realities. Each person embarking on this path of schooling in the right way will also contribute to the health of his social context. 'Spiritual science should make us practical, immediately practical, more practical than so-called pragmatists imagine.'[4]

Thinking—a means to understand the world

'Anyone who wants to work within life must first understand life. Here lies the essence of the matter.'[5] Steiner's work in this field inevitably started with him establishing the methodological foundations of a theory of knowledge:

> Badly built bridges collapse; and it is then clear even to the most prejudiced person that the bridge builder is a bungler. But how is it with all that is botched in the social context? This becomes apparent in the fact that our fellow men suffer from it.[6]

If an engineer bungles, it has direct, visible consequences. How much daily bungling is done by our social theorists, social practitioners, and party politicians? The consequences do not so clearly point to their causes. A sensitive person notices only continual suffering in people around him—which erodes human vitality.

It is interesting that, again and again, new generations take a stand against this suffering. Their parents and teachers have—ultimately—resigned themselves to this permanent state of misery, a status quo which is often enforced by external laws and even military might. But new generations emerging into earthly life from the holy fire of the spiritual world can erupt forcefully if they discover hardened social conditions or an intellectual life that suppresses impulses of renewal. Resulting outbreaks of violence can culminate in precisely the opposite of what lived in their original, pure impulse.

In the last third of the previous century, in particular, such impulses and movements arose with great power and impetus. The young generation experienced the distress and suffering of the very people who lived in outer, material abundance. They had a strong sense of injustice and a distinct quality of compassion. But what they lacked was clear awareness of humanity's condition. Their faculty of thinking was rooted in intellectual learning. And they became rightly suspicious of this cold intellectuality. Because they could not find a way of thinking adequate to life, either in art or in academic culture, neither could they easily find ways to fulfil their own destiny—something they so desperately sought. The theories they had been taught had nothing to do with life itself but were stale ideologies that had been carried over to our modern times from the past, at best from the 19th century, or still earlier, from the Middle Ages.

'Anyone who wants to work within life must first understand life.... Right action arises from right thinking; and wrong action arises from wrong thinking, or from lack of thought.'[7] This lack of thought, or abstract thinking that no longer finds access to reality, still governs modern existence in all kinds of ways.

A new, true understanding of exploitation

In his second article, Steiner continued by explaining that the principle of exploitation is not dependent on being poor or rich:

> ... but rather, whether I am rich or poor, it is only a matter of whether or not I pay the worker enough when he produces the dress

for me. I exploit others when I buy things from workers who have not been properly paid.[8]

One cannot really describe the problem of exploitation better than this. In the framework of our present economic system, each one of us is a consumer who strives to purchase things at as low a price as possible.

Consciousness of the fact that everyone who does not pay a just price participates in an unsocial system could create a feeling of responsibility in every consumer. Our social ills today are based on the consumer's inability to properly 'value' the producer's products or work. Many products, especially those produced in the non-industrial processes of agriculture, or in developing countries and newly emerging economies, are offered on the market at far too low a price. Often, it is the suffering and the hardship of the producers that lie unseen in their products. Not to mention the children deprived of their childhood so that products can be produced more cheaply. Alongside this, the fabric of nature is being recklessly damaged. If consumers stopped purchasing such products they would quickly disappear from the market.

But exploitation goes still further. When a consumer purchases an apple produced on an industrial scale, sprayed with pesticides, he contributes to promotion of an agribusiness that is hostile to life in so many ways. At the same time, a biodynamic farmer who lovingly works his land in connection with the earth, nature, animals and consumers, cannot sell his products because consumers do not want to pay the price that corresponds to the value of these products. Understanding how exploitation makes all of us complicit also calls upon all of us to work together to overcome these conditions. It would be a great step forward for our society if only the products that the consumer truly, consciously wanted were produced.

The fundamental social law

Rudolf Steiner then proceeded to formulate the fundamental social law, which is diametrically opposed to the basic principle that Adam Smith formulated. According to Adam Smith, a society will function all the better, the more that each individual lives out of his egotism. True, Adam Smith does not express this in such direct language. At the beginning of Smith's primary work on ethics, he wrote:

> No matter how much one may perceive the human being as being very egotistical, there are certain evident principles in his nature that direct him to take part in the destiny of others.[9]

Nevertheless, he saw egotism as the incentive for all economic advancement.

In his view, if everyone who participates in the activities of the market lives out of their maximum self-interest, then an invisible hand will reverse this effect to create a 'benefit to all'. Yet anyone who observes the actual activities of the markets today, especially in the 20th century, can experience the absurdity of Smith's thoughts on the matter. Actual developments have shown that the free operation of competition in the markets leads only to the result that the rich and powerful players in the market become ever richer and more powerful, and the 'powerless' are kept so. Because these ideas, even today, hold such fascination for people—indeed, even a magic potency—the overwhelming majority of people today consciously or unconsciously base their thinking on this ideology. And in consequence humanity, and all the developments that humanity has achieved since the Age of Enlightenment, fall by the wayside.

Naturally, egotism is also an undeniable part of human nature. Failing to recognize this drive in human beings would leave us blind to reality. Most social theoreticians, and so-called social pragmatists even more so, conclude that society must therefore ensure that each person receives as much income from his own productivity as possible.

Rudolf Steiner, working out of his unprejudiced and ideology-free research mode, which he developed from Goethe's phenomenological method and based on his own spiritual-scientific foundations, comes to precisely the opposite insight:

> The health of a whole group of human beings working together is all the greater, the less that each individual takes the proceeds of his own work for himself—in other words, the more that the proceeds of his work are given over to his fellow workers, and the more that his own needs are met not from his own productive work, but rather are satisfied from the productive work done by others. All arrangements within a collective of human beings that contradict this law, must, over the course of time, create need and hardship somewhere.[11]

One should not speak of right and wrong in the social realm. It is much more appropriate to speak of health or illness. Naturally, there are also basic principles to be considered within the social realm. If one does not consider them, then the social organism will become ill over time and 'create need and hardship'.

Every community must find its own form: there is no single right or wrong one, but instead we must respect the basic lawfulness inherent in the social realm. And when such laws are not adhered to, 'all arrangements will, over time, create need and hardship somewhere' in society. We can immediately see that poorly done engineering work produces poor quality—and perhaps dangerous—streets, buildings or bridges. Most people do not observe the same as quickly in the realm of social interaction.

Steiner gave initial indications about how the social reality of this law can be realized. It is a law that is naturally and comprehensively active in every community that functions through a division of labour.

Wherever human beings work on behalf of the needs of other human beings, economic values arise and are brought into economic circulation. Goods and services can then be valued, and also paid for, but payment should never be for an individual's skills and capacities, nor for working hours as an abstract assessment of the time taken in work for others.

> Within the economic realm, only the value of the goods is at issue. In this realm, the performance of services, which proceed from the spirit ... also take on the character of goods. One can as little pay the worker for his capacity to work, as pay a teacher for his individual capacities. Both of them can only be paid for what they produce as commodities and goods that enter into economic circulation.[12]

Here, we already have an overview of the idea of the threefold social organism that Rudolf Steiner presented after the First World War. A person's capacities live completely within the realm of his intellectual, spiritual and cultural activity. The production of commodities or performing of services belong to the realm of economic life. Binding contracts, and all agreements—including work contracts, conditions of work, and agreements about payment for work—all belong to the realm of rights: 'This law holds true for social life in the same absolute way and with the same necessity that any law of nature has in relation to any realm of actual natural causation.'

It is essential to create institutions

In elaborating this fundamental social law, Steiner was quick to anticipate potential misunderstandings and objections. It was not a matter of having this law serve only as a 'general moral law', as a way of thinking that people could adopt:

> No. In reality, this law only lives as it should when a collective of human beings succeeds in creating institutions such that no one can

ever claim the fruits of their own work for themselves, but rather—as far as is possible—these are given without reserve to serve the benefit of the whole collective. Each must, in turn, receive benefit from the work of his fellow human beings. What matters is that the work done for others and the remuneration or payment received are two completely separate things.[13]

This fundamental social law continues to be misunderstood today—being still regarded as a moral exhortation. In fact, Rudolf Steiner was speaking here of an objective social law that simply exists in our present world, without any regard to our moral disposition.

Rudolf Steiner depicted how a transition out of 'social egotism' can and must proceed through a revision of our working relations. As long as people are held in 'wage labour' they can only degenerate into egotism. Economic value-creation occurs at the level of economic life, whereas the receiving of remuneration occurs at a very different level, that of human dignity, and thus within the sphere of the rights life, to which all human beings belong through their entitlement to equality. In line with this, it becomes possible for the first time for people freely to place their capacities at the disposal of their fellow men, in selflessness, to serve the highest good on earth. This enables conditions for a free spiritual/cultural life to be met—and simultaneously conditions for solidarity and fraternity in economic life. 'It must become possible for each person voluntarily to pursue his calling, to the measure of his ability.'[14]

Conditions for realization of the fundamental social law

A prerequisite for creating such conditions is that each individual experiences itself as a part of the whole. The whole community will thereby cultivate the sense of a common objective, a common task, a mission. Each must feel himself part of this whole and a participant in these common objectives. This consciousness of purpose, the conscious experience of the value of the whole, will increasingly replace self-interest and the egotism of the past. But naturally, self-determination also belongs to this, and must underpin social structure and interaction. 'The whole must have a spiritual mission; and each individual must want to contribute so that the mission will be fulfilled.'[15] Steiner left completely open the size that this whole must have. I think that this too, will be a path of development. Initially, these communities will certainly have the small scale of a 'like-minded' family. Subsequently they will expand into work associations, then into 'business relationships'; and in future the dimensions can grow to encompass, ultimately, the whole of humanity.

The social theories of the 19th and 20th centuries have not created any new foundations for society. More or less everyone has remained in thrall to materialism. Such theories can indeed generate short-term actions, but cannot engender real health.

> The only thing that can help is a spiritual world view, which, through itself, through what it has to offer, establishes itself in the thoughts, feeling, will, in short, in the whole soul of the human being.[16]

Rudolf Steiner made clear in his introductory comments on the fundamental social law that progress could not happen without developing a new thinking about our relationships. But thinking, for him, should not be misunderstood as something purely abstract. Instead it is a conscious way to receive the fire of spirit. This fire can then warm mankind's feelings and ignite the will, transforming society so that it begins to bear a human countenance.

To find the motivation to work on behalf of another person, I need a fair-minded view of this other. Not until I have also seen the other person's being in its higher sense, come to know its spiritual source, will I find in this entelechy the basis to act for my own highest good in harmony with my destiny. This future objective and purpose can be understood as placing our work at the service of others, as sacrifice. But this absolutely requires 'a world view that acts according to true knowledge of the spirit.'[17]

On this basis, each will also know his social task, regardless of what his social standing is. Each can contribute, in his own way, to the future objectives of humanity. And thereby it is possible for the deepest feelings and impulses to arise and form the basis for the future health of social relations. When human beings infuse themselves with the right consciousness and feelings, social actions—which naturally always include the striving to consider other individuals—will be felt to be as necessary as food and drink. And a person will then find his own place, and the place of his community, in the framework of the social whole: '... and so the single-spirit of this community will coalesce into an image full of spiritual purpose, of the unified mission of the whole of humankind.'[18]

Naturally, we are only just starting out on this path, this spiritual movement. It will 'need to develop into its higher spiritual mission'. It must and can become a wellspring for social awareness and social actions.

Humanity can only progress when the members of this movement become ever more conscious of their social responsibility and fulfil their social mission.

> This advancement of humanity can only come about if we create the real conditions for it. And these conditions cannot be brought about in any other way than by one individual after another finding their way to it. The world takes a step forward only when the human being wills it.[19]

The third article ends with the words, 'There are some who shall soon take this still further.' At that time, in 1906, there was no real interest in these ideas and impulses in theosophical circles. It was for this reason that Rudolf Steiner did not continue writing on this theme after the third article, for

> ... this would have only had a meaning if it had been taken up in a practical way, and had been acted upon. Because it has been entirely disregarded, I have ceased pursuing it for the time being, and have not brought it up again. One must certainly hope that these things will meet with ever greater understanding.[20]

Only after the First World War, between 1917 and 1919, when Rudolf Steiner was once again asked questions on this theme, did he begin to offer further remarks on the subject. In the many lectures and articles that he developed to present the ideas of the *threefold social organism*, we find a description of social reality as the foundation for practically realizing the 'fundamental social law' within society.

In responding to actual circumstances, Steiner formulated the need for creating 'a healthy consumer association, not one blindly and haphazardly established ... out of arbitrary ideas and predilections.'[21]

Interest in others

Rudolf Steiner demonstrated that our capacities are the fruits of previous earthy lives. Through division of labour, the principle of fraternity becomes the shaping element in economic relationships. Division of labour and specialization, and also mechanization and virtualization in the production process, require, however, a further element: interest in the other human being. When we carry out our activities for the needs of another, we realize a deep impulse for the future: interest in the other, love that is realized in a free deed, becomes an impulse that shapes the future and will give rise to new conditions on earth in future.

However, any kind of work for wages hinders such impulses for a future humanity. Rudolf Steiner stated this repeatedly and radically:

> Indeed, real, fundamental conviction regarding reincarnation and karma can never flourish in a world where people consider that wages and work must directly correspond, and where it is thought that we must earn the necessaries of life in exact proportion to our work.[22]

Interest in our fellow man will increasingly replace interest in ourselves. However, this requires a world view that encompasses the spiritual nature of the human being.

Division of labour, caring for others and a comprehensive and collective method of production are the principles of modern economic organization. Today, no region of the earth is able to supply all its own needs. Only comprehensive, global cooperation can properly meet post-industrial conditions of production. In the 21st century, directing our activity to serve other persons or groups of people also requires the economically functional principle of solidarity or *fraternity* in our collaborative working.

The streams of economic values are accompanied by rights processes: working individuals are obliged to collaborate, and consumers are entitled to acquire the commodities produced. These rights processes are mediated by money. Money as a rights element, therefore, regulates our rights relationships. The monetary system, as our collective rights life, must be placed on a democratic foundation. In this way, rights processes can be shaped within a new mode of collaboration based on the measure of *equality*.

Freedom—equality—fraternity

Freedom, equality and fraternity are the functional principles of a modern community built on self-regulation. Such a community is only 'human-scale', in Steiner's view, when it is structured in a threefold way: freedom in spiritual/cultural life, equality in the rights life, and fraternity in economic life.

Threefolding of the social organism, the most pressing need of our times, would address the aspirations of modern humanity and create a basis for gradual realization of the fundamental social law, with all its implications.

Not until the three realms—spiritual/cultural life 'based on human capacities', economic life involving the production, distribution, and consumption of commodities, and the rights life, concerned with the relationships between people—are each established independently, and each shaped and governed by their own, different laws and conditions, will social life be able to unfold in a healthy way. The fundamental social law needs a tripartite social organism to become reality, in which 'working for our fellow human beings and receiving a certain income are two completely separate things'.

Each of us belongs to a particular community, organized by human rights, and is entitled to an income that makes it possible for us to have a dignified livelihood and thus live in dignity. Only where there is such a foundation, where the community guarantees this basis for life to all, will it be possible for a person to commit himself to investing his own unique capacities in his work in productive service to the community—completely out of his own free will. Income thus becomes a right based on our belonging to a productive society. Work, by contrast, results from the individual initiative of each individual, within the context of a labour-divided whole. Thus, work and income become two 'completely separate' things in the context of a modern, labour-divided method of production. And so, our task in the present time becomes clear: to recognize and to understand the fundamental social law as it relates to the threefold social organism; to explore as many different approaches as possible, with artistic variations in different social contexts; and make both insights and practical experiences accessible to the widest possible circle of people. This is also how such a foundational law can be realized within our social realities, within the foreseeable future, in the actual world.

Notes

1. Rudolf Steiner, *Knowledge of the Higher Worlds*, Rudolf Steiner Press 2004, p. 212.
2. Rudolf Steiner, articles in *Lucifer* and *Lucifer-Gnosis* magazines 1903–1908. GA 34, p. 191 [German edition]. *Anthroposophy and the Social Question*, Mercury Press, Spring Valley 1996.
3. Rudolf Steiner, op. cit., GA 34, p. 193.
4. Rudolf Steiner in a lecture in Berlin on 12 October 1905: *Unsere Weltlage, Krieg, Frieden und die Wissenschaft des Geistes*, ['The present situation in the world; war, peace, and spiritual science'], GA 54, p. 35.
5. Rudolf Steiner, op. cit., GA 34, p. 194.
6. Ibid., p. 195.
7. Ibid., p. 206.
8. Ibid., p. 16.

9. Adam Smith, *The Theory of Moral Sentiments*, Glasgow 1759.
10. Adam Smith, *An Inquiry Into the Nature and Causes of the Wealth of Nations*, Book 1, Chapter 2, London 1776.
11. Rudolf Steiner, op. cit., GA 34, p. 213.
12. Rudolf Steiner, *Die Kernpunkte der Sozialen Frage* (published in English as *Towards Social Renewal*, Rudolf Steiner Press 1999), GA 23, Dornach 1976, p. 130.
13. Rudolf Steiner, op. cit., GA 34, p. 213.
14. Rudolf Steiner, op. cit. GA 34, p. 216.
15. Ibid., p. 215.
16. Ibid., p. 217.
17. Ibid., p. 28.
18. Ibid., p. 31.
19. Ibid., p. 32.
20. Rudolf Steiner, *World Economy*, Rudolf Steiner Press, London, 1972, GA 340, p. 38.
21. Rudolf Steiner, 14.04.1919, *Vergangenheits und Zukunftsimpulse im sozialen Geschehen*, GA 190, Dornach 1980.
22. Rudolf Steiner, lecture of 21.2.1912, *Wiederverkörperung und Karma*, GA 135, Dornach 1989, p. 88.

6. The Middle Realm of Social Life—the Rights Sphere as Our Earthly Task

Distressing inconsistency

We live in a time full of contradictions. For example, the 'fundamental social law' as formulated by Rudolf Steiner turns on its head everything that liberalism has taught us. It is actually a matter-of-fact description of what the workforce portion of society and the economy have created. No one can any longer work only for him- or herself. Everything that I bring forth in terms of work is for others, and comes about in connection with others. The baker bakes bread least of all for himself and his family (though he may also do that) but largely for others: the consumers. Other people have built his house or provided his clothing, food, car, etc. It's always reciprocal—each person works for others. As single person we are becoming increasingly individual—yet our community life requires increasing social interaction.

Here we experience the polarity—the contradictory nature—of our modern economy. On the one hand it is organized in an altruistic way, with each person working for others. Yet on the other hand the idea has been inculcated in us that people should act out of self-interest, that everyone should be egotistic, since this moves society forward. This results in the schizophrenia in which we live. I believe that this is a great source of illness for people in our time—that what they think with their head is different from what they actually feel in their heart and enact with their will. This inconsistency is distressing and destructive.

The incarnation spiral

Here is a drawing of two spirals (see p. 65), which together enclose a middle realm. Along the incarnation spiral, the soul comes from prenatal existence and brings impulses into earthly life—intentions for what he or she wishes to realize in this life. In many different contexts, Rudolf Steiner describes how the 'achievements' of our previous incarnation flow into capacities and tasks that we bring down to earth from pre-birth, in order to develop and realize them here. In our society, we refer to everything that has to do with these intrinsic human capacities as spiritual life—in realms such as education, which is often specifically mentioned, but in many others too. This spiritual life, these capacities that we bring with us, need to be able to unfold and develop **freely**. Steiner describes exactly when and how this is hindered. The moment I have to sell my labour in exchange for payment, this incarnation process is no longer possible in a healthy way: '... It is not heaven but hell that we would create on earth if the human race were ruled by nothing other than competition, compulsive acquisitiveness...'[1]

The excarnation spiral

Opposite the incarnation spiral we have the excarnation spiral. Here, too, Rudolf Steiner describes quite clearly what happens on this path. What we bring from pre-birth has to come to realization in collaboration with other human beings—in economic life—and needs to unfold in fraternity. There are grounds for obstruction here as well: If we don't work together out of solidarity, if we don't turn lovingly to the person in need, but instead work out of egotism and greed for profit, then the unfolding of fraternity—our earthly mission—is hampered. Just as, on the one hand, the incarnation stream is encumbered by working for payment, so also the healthy excarnation process is obstructed by greed for profit, by egotistical economic activity. Rudolf Steiner is very radical and totally clear about this: it doesn't just get a little worse; it is prevented! Only what takes place with loving attention towards—and in solidarity with—another human being has meaning for the higher hierarchies, for the spiritual world. Since these higher hierarchies have released human beings into freedom and can no longer directly influence them, they rely on the human being to develop these qualities out of himself. Steiner tells us that by conscious and selfless activity of this kind for our sisters and brothers, we are preparing a future planetary stage of the earth, the Jupiter stage. This question has concerned me for several years. For me this is basically why it is imperative for someone in our time to concern himself with the social question, with the economic question and with the separation of work and income.

The middle realm—our true earthly task

The reason we incarnate is to meet other human beings and create rights. This is our earthly task! The sphere in which this takes place is the rights sphere, this middle realm to which the principle of equality and fairness, or justice, belongs. Working for a wage can be eliminated through rights regulation. We need regulations that prevent pure egotism in our economic life from gaining ascendancy, and which, on the contrary, make it possible for people's activity to serve one another fraternally. Rights alone don't bring this about, but this realm creates the conditions enabling us to act in freedom, in a fraternal way.

THE MIDDLE REALM OF SOCIAL LIFE

In the polarity between spiritual life and economic life, the rights sphere lies between the two. It lives in the relation of one person to another, and is experienced particularly in the spirit of language. All social elements have their origin between birth and death, and therefore exist within immediate reality. The modern life of the state can be based only on a foundation of democracy, and must always be governed by principles of human dignity and equality. But the valuing of work, its regulation, protection and scope, likewise belongs to the rights sphere.

Threefolding of the social organism requires a living grasp of the inner lawfulness of social processes—but not in a dogmatic form that, say, equates private schools with the sphere of spiritual life, the police force and parliament with the rights sphere, and the school cafeteria to economic life. Besides considering separate institutions, we should also try to see the interconnectedness of phenomena, and the laws at work in them in daily life.

Every entrepreneurial activity and actually every economic activity—including working on an assembly line—has its origin, according to Rudolf Steiner, in spiritual life. Capacities are called for—they may have to be developed—for this activity to take place at all. Another person endowed with other capacities can't accomplish this same task. The way a teacher meets the needs of his students or their parents naturally falls into the domain of 'value' and is thereby part of the economy. The rights

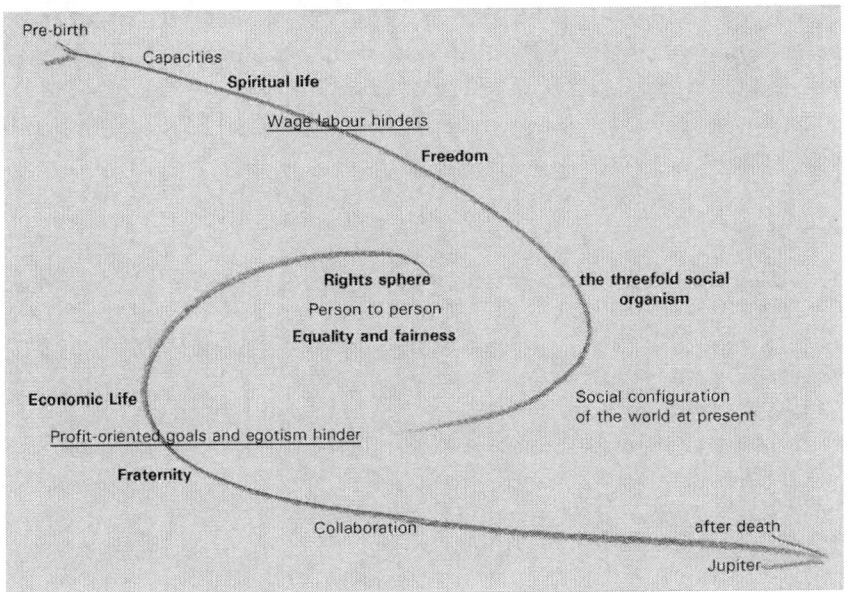

sphere is directly connected with what is earthly, with our actual earthly task. It is our responsibility to configure this realm democratically throughout the world, in such a way that we invoke fraternity, the human element. We have to become increasingly conscious of this.

Spiritual dimensions of threefolding

To conclude I would like to quote something which Rudolf Steiner said in a lecture in Stuttgart in 1912.[2]

> You see, nothing has such an adverse effect on real convictions about reincarnation and karma as the principle that we should earn a wage directly corresponding to the work we have done ... Increasingly we should realize that a world order in which it is thought that work and wages must directly correspond to each other—in which, so to speak, one has to earn by one's work what one needs to live—will never allow a fully grounded conviction about reincarnation and karma to thrive.

Rudolf Steiner could scarcely have put it more radically than this. So long as people think that they work for their money, they can never gain an understanding of reincarnation and karma. We have to bring the social question into this dimension. We cannot progress in our spiritual development and fulfil our earthly task '... without arranging the social organism in a threefold way: in the sense of fraternity in economic life, democracy in the life of the state or rights sphere, and freedom or individualism in spiritual life. This has to be seen as the only way to heal and rescue humanity ...'[3] Yet a society of this kind can never be dictated by state regulations, but arises only through the free collaboration and cooperation of human individuals.

Notes

1. Rudolf Steiner, *The Karma of Vocation*, GA 172, lecture of 12 November 1916.
2. Rudolf Steiner, *Reincarnation and Karma—Two Fundamental Truths of Human Existence*, GA 135, lecture of 21 February 1912.
3. Rudolf Steiner, lecture of 9 August 1919, Dornach, in *Education as a Social Problem* (1984), later published as *Education As a Force for Social Change* (1997), GA 296.

7. Rudolf Steiner's World Economy and the Goethean Research Method

Describing his methodology for research, knowledge and insight into economics, Rudolf Steiner states the following:

> Economics needs a descriptive method of thinking, which sets out from different starting points, allowing them to culminate in concepts... Descriptive economics is only possible if one enters into the phenomena with one's thinking, especially as in economics one is constantly working from the past into the future... I very carefully tried to give guidelines, examples, illustrations... In economics one should not abstract something from the totality of phenomena, but should arrive at it through this totality... But one must be aware of the fact that economic thinking must be more or less total, a thinking of a very comprehensive kind...[1]

Rudolf Steiner here applies Goethe's research method to the social and economic realm. He suggests that this method is the means, the path, we ourselves have to pursue. Thus he offers us a signpost towards further exploration and insight.

Goethe describes his method very clearly and briefly in the preface to his *Theory of Colours*:

> In reality, any attempt to express the inner nature of a thing is fruitless. What we perceive are effects, and a complete record of these effects ought to encompass this inner nature. We labour in vain to describe a person's character, but when we compile his actions, his deeds, a picture of his character will emerge. Colours are the deeds of light, what it does and what it endures. In this sense we can expect them to tell us something about light...[2]

Rudolf Steiner always practised his scientific method in the Goethean sense, by considering the totality of his subject. He compiled all the effects, the impressions that he perceived. In this way he assembles a work of art, and in this composed totality the spectator can also experience the essence, the inner being of what is observed. Initially we may not understand all parts of this composition, but we may use them as signposts to find our way to the spirit, to the inner essence of phenomena. We can describe the aim of this research method as follows: perceiving a phenomenon that appears in the world such that its concept, its lawfulness, the idea living within it, can be brought into expression in cognitive thinking. To experience this idea within reality, 'is true human communion' between the world and ourselves.[3]

Only by practising this method ourselves will we be able to understand Rudolf Steiner's lectures and courses. This becomes apparent in the first step taken in his economics course, in the way he formulates an understanding of economic value:

> An economic value, seen from this one aspect, is a natural product transformed by human labour... One value-forming factor is human labour, which transforms a natural product so as to introduce it into economic circulation ...

Then comes a second aspect:

> Here we have the second aspect of value-forming factors in economics. Here labour stands in the background, and before it the spirit which directs and governs the labour. Labour shines through the spirit, and this again creates an economic value.[4]

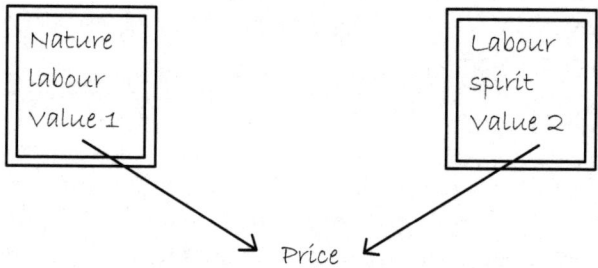

In value 1 we have 'labour applied to nature' and in value 2, 'spirit applied to labour'. This means, in the first case, that labour is directing the process of transforming nature, giving rise to economic value 1; and in the second case, spirit directs and transforms labour, thus creating economic value 2.

Rudolf Steiner gives us a very important and precise description of work:

> Work, in the economic sense, begins when human beings produce for one another... Work arises when nature is transformed by the human being for the purpose of being consumed... Work is a human activity expended on a natural product to render it con-

sumable... By (means of) intelligence one can share out this work, but the resulting structuring of work distances itself from the product. It is a mere division of labour.[5]

This makes it very clear that only work done for the needs of consumers is work in the sense illustrated in Rudolf Steiner's economics course. And it also shows that the directing of work can be a purely spiritual deed, manifesting in the labour applied to transforming matter.

In lecture 4 we grasp that the modern economy is a functional system. This means that economic processes are both value-creating and value-destroying; they are organic life processes, composing and decomposing; and we have to perceive this from different points of view. We must not fix our point of view in a dogmatic way. We need to practise continual mobility and metamorphosis of all concepts. By these means we can ultimately experience the spiritual content, the idea. But this needs to be a flexible, living thinking.

From here, lectures 5, 6 and 7 take us through further steps concerning the economic processes. We find here the three factors of production: Nature—Work—Spirit (capital)*

Steiner speaks of the 'loan character of industrial capital'. And we find these elements are related to the concepts of purchase—loan—gift; and also: commodity (goods)—means of production—industrial capital.†

In lecture 7, Rudolf Steiner observes the steps from a barter economy to an economy of faculties (abilities). There is a metamorphosis that occurs between a bartering economy and a money economy, and a further metamorphosis to arrive at an economy of human faculties or capacities. This economy of faculties is where we actually find ourselves today, but our thinking and our concepts still remain in the past, corresponding only to the structure of a bartering economy.

The essential point is that we have a new structure in the economic realm: the production side and the consumption side have developed into a polar form. This polarity highlights two different processes and concepts for the production side and the consumption side. The concepts we use in our economic life still belong to the time before and of Adam Smith, concepts built up in relation to a barter economy, including concepts of private property, which are only adequate for the one side, that of the private domain of the consumer. In the realm of production in modern times, with its elaborated division of labour, it

---

* Christopher Houghton Budd translates these as: land, labour, capital.
† CHB: land, labour, intelligence.

makes no sense to speak of property, whether private, collective or mutual. The means of production are part of the total system of production, and the individual or group with the best capacities or faculties uses them to produce what it creates for other people. To be healthy, an economy of faculties has to enable the means of production to keep moving around to the person or the group with the best faculties and mode of application.

And this is the most decisive task for entrepreneurial activity: to direct capital to the individual or the group with the best capability and efficiency. Here again we find three concepts, discovering that 1) purchase money has metamorphosed into a loan of working capital in order to produce consumer goods; 2) loan money has metamorphosed into investment capital for producing the means of production; and 3) surplus money created through production has metamorphosed into subsidies, grants or gifts to social or public welfare enterprises such as schools, hospitals, or environmental regeneration etc. I think it is fundamental to differentiate the processes or occurrences now found in a modern, entrepreneurial economy from ones belonging to bygone days, to an earlier time with an economy based on barter.

In lecture 11, we are told that the development of economic life 'consists of a series of successive stages, in which, however, the earlier stages continue to exist side by side with the later'. In line with the trinity of barter—loan—gift described in lecture 12, Rudolf Steiner highlights three functions of money, which he terms purchase money, loan money and gift money. He relates how loan money gradually transforms through economic processes to become gift money, where it then loses its value, depreciates. You may understand the sense of this remark if you look at the circulation of money in Beuys's blackboard drawings following money's continuous development. (See illustration by Joseph Beuys, The Capital Space 1970–1977, in Chapter 2, p. 22.)

Investment capital is given to the gifted and able entrepreneur, who will rationalize production and make it more efficient, creating increasing benefit which can be given to enterprises in the cultural realm, and to welfare enterprises. All developed countries already practise this, but they do not have the concepts or insights to understand this new reality. And inadequate concepts will never give rise to adequate precautions and actions. Since the required steps are not taken, ever more explosive social situations arise. The financial crisis has emerged as a consequence of misguided and inadequate concepts for the monetary system. The signposts given in Rudolf Steiner's economic courses already point to this situation: industrial money has to be transformed into gift money to serve the cultural life.

In this context we also can discuss the notion of 'old money' and 'new money' in the twelfth lecture of the course. We have new or 'young' money when we are initiating new enterprises or new productive concepts. This is money given to the creative entrepreneur. We have old money when the money has lost its direct relation to any economic value, and economic values are cancelled. Old money has to flow back to the central banking system where it originated. Rudolf Steiner also describes this aspect of money in the Discourses, where he mentions that we can give an ageing character to money by using a bill of exchange. He illustrates this as follows:

> This means that money has to age. It is merely a question of how to do this. Now, one can only give outer reality to the gradual devaluation of money by date-stamping it; these stamped notes [which

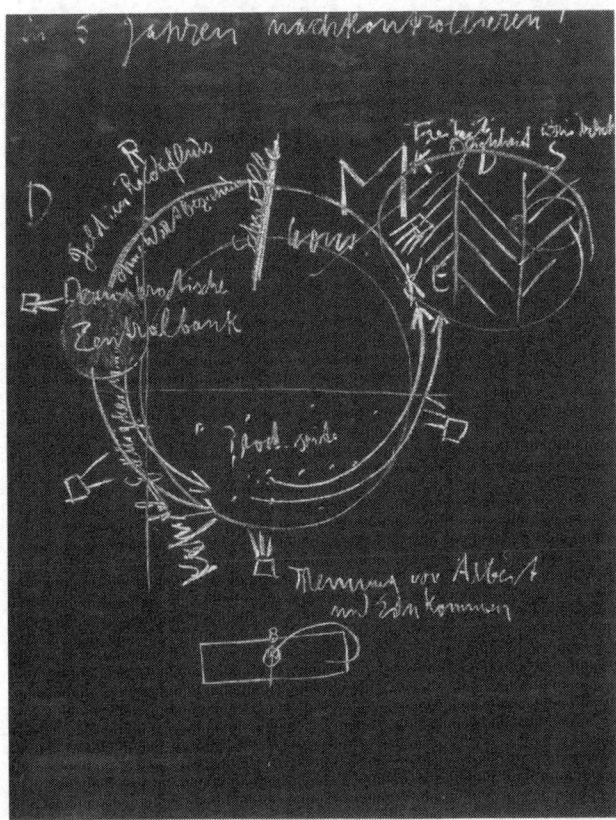

Blackboard sketch by Joseph Beuys depicting money circulation, 'Please check after five years!' The Capital Space 1970–1977, Hallen für Neue Kunst, Schaffhausen, Switzerland

> expire at a certain date] are processed by officials. But this requires a very complicated bureaucracy. So rather than external devaluation, we must guide money through the real course of economic events. This can be done by first giving all types of money the form of a bill (of exchange), that is, by means of an expiry date.[6]

This again shows how fruitful it can be to engage with the content of Steiner's course with our own active thinking. Only when we look behind or inside the world of outward appearance can we experience the underlying ideas, the spiritual world. Only concepts that originate in life's core realities can be a source of sustainable change.

Wherever we try to shed light on passages in the course that are unclear to us, the living concepts we are trying to make visible to ourselves will prove their fruitfulness if we approach them with the right kind of thinking. At the end of lecture 12 is stated:

> Perhaps you will say that this is hard to follow. It is... This, however, should really be our task. All that can be said in the present lectures should be taken as a basis for further research in economics. In the brief period of a fortnight, only hints and suggestions can be given; but you will find that all the economic statements which have been made here will be transformed by detailed investigation into valuable economic truths—valuable both in theory and in practice.[7]

In lecture 14, Rudolf Steiner emphasizes how he tried to find pictorial concepts, ideal pictures to aid the participants 'in making proper use of the wide range of valuable material... Such a feeling is inevitable, for life will not endure dogmatic theories; and it is in this sense that the ideal pictures I have given to you need to be conceived.'[8] In the discourses he also offers a very interesting close to these considerations:

> Pure money loses its value. If we grasped such things with our common sense we would do less harm. That is why I am not concerned to agitate, but to draw attention to realities, to things that are already there to be seen. In this way world economy can be helped to healthy expression.[9]

Most of the lectures in Rudolf Steiner's Economics Course end with similar remarks, an exploration of which is beyond the scope of this essay. Engaging with these issues practically is work that must be undertaken by responsible groups, and cannot be done in an abstract way. 'Associations', as Steiner calls them, are groups designed to discuss all matters arising between producers, consumers and distributors, between companies in vertical and horizontal relationships. Such groups will create a new culture of conversation and social entrepreneurship.

For many years, mainly in Central Europe, Rudolf Steiner's approach to world economy was studied very dogmatically. Advocates were so impressed by Rudolf Steiner's accomplishments that they did not dare to develop their own self-reliant, independent thinking. But the latter is precisely what our modern times require. We can recognize two individuals in the 20th century who worked innovatively towards what will be needed in the 21st century: Wilhelm Schmundt and Joseph Beuys.

The first, Wilhelm Schmundt, had wide experience in the economic realm, as an organizer of electrical supply and a manager of several power plants in East Prussia. He later worked in a Waldorf school as a physics teacher. He was also a social scientist in the Social Science Section at the Goetheanum—a very fine representative of Goethean research methodology. The second, Joseph Beuys, the renowned German artist, working in the second half of the 20th century, was an activist and advocate for the threefold social organism. Beuys admired Schmundt as 'our great teacher'.

It is not easy to understand and practise this Goethean path of cognition and its phenomenological method, but by doing so we can experience freedom in knowing and action illumined by a thinking methodology that is entirely modern and, in my view, extremely valuable. But a second step has to be added when we approach the social realm. A large enough number of people must come into association with each other if they want to change conditions in the world. Our world urgently needs to change to safeguard humanity's continuing survival. So let us seek to practise this new approach to thinking, and let us join together in social groups that are willing to work towards a new world: let us create living social sculpture together.

> Indeed, there are many reasons why this age of a money economy has ended.* And it cannot be vanquished, either through democracy or through legal measures, or through the economy itself, as Karl Marx thought it could. Instead it can be overcome only through the concept of art. But an art that relates to the abilities of all human beings. Only then will we come to real culture again. And much work has already been done in this direction. *Joseph Beuys*

Notes

1. Rudolf Steiner, *Economics*, New Economy Publications 1996, GA 341, pp. 179–186.
2. Goethe, *Scientific Studies VII*, Suhrkamp, New York 1988, 'Physics', Preface, p. 138.
3. Rudolf Steiner, *Goethean Science*, Mercury Press, Spring Valley 1988, p. 91.
4. Rudolf Steiner, *World Economy*, Rudolf Steiner Press, London 1972, pp. 31–32.

    Editor's note: *Labour shines through the spirit* refers directly to an example that Rudolf Steiner gave a moment before in the lecture, describing how a background colour can be overlaid by another colour but will still shine through it—showing something of itself, but changed by what now covers it. Thus spirit overlays labour, and labour now shines through that spirit, as if from beneath it, expressing itself in a new way, in a new hue.
5. Rudolf Steiner, 'Discourses' (in *Economics*, op. cit.) GA 341, p. 209.
6. Rudolf Steiner, 'Discourses' (in *Economics*, op. cit.) p. 220.
7. Rudolf Steiner, *Economics*, op. cit., p. 155.
8. Rudolf Steiner, *Economics*, op. cit., p. 166.
9. Rudolf Steiner, 'Discourses' (in *Economics*, op. cit.), p. 222.

---

*Translator: Beuys means here that a money economy is no longer appropriate, that we need to progress beyond it.

8. The Biodynamic Farm and the Social Organism:

Lecture given at a conference in Chennai, Amethyst in December 2012 on 'Saving the Earth as a Healthy Organism'

The invitation to this conference included the following quotations:
Sri Aurobindo, in: *The Ideal of Human Unity—The religion of humanity: liberty, equality and fraternity*[1]

> ... *For that essentially must be the aim of the religion of humanity, as it must be the earthly aim of all human religion. Love, mutual recognition of human brotherhood, a living sense of human oneness and practice of human oneness in thought, feeling and life, the ideal which was expressed first some thousands of years ago in the ancient Vedic hymn (Rig Veda 10. 191) and must always remain the highest injunction of the Spirit within us to human life upon earth ...*
>
> *The aim of the religion of humanity was formulated in the eighteenth century by a sort of primal intuition; that aim was and it is still to recreate human society in the image of three kindred ideas: liberty, equality and fraternity. None of these has really been won in spite of all the progress that has been achieved ... It has laboured to establish a political, social and legal liberty, equality and mutual help in an equal association.*
>
> *But although these aims are of great importance in their own field, they are not the central thing; they can only be secure when founded upon a change of the inner human nature and inner way of living; they are themselves of importance only as a means for giving a greater scope and a better field for man's development towards that change and, when it is once achieved, as an outward expression of a larger inward life. <u>Freedom, equality, brotherhood are three godheads of the soul</u>; they cannot be really achieved through the external machinery of society or by man so long as he lives only in the individual and the communal ego. When the ego claims liberty, it arrives at a competitive individualism. When it asserts equality, it arrives first at strife, then at an attempt to ignore the variations of Nature and, as the sole way of doing that successfully, it constructs an artificial and machine-made society. A society that pursues liberty as its ideal is unable to achieve equality; a society that aims at equality will be obliged to sacrifice liberty. For the ego to speak of fraternity is for it to speak of something contrary to its nature. All that it knows is association for the pursuit of common egoistic ends and the utmost it can arrive at is a closer organization for the equal distribution of labour, production, consumption and enjoyment.*

> *Yet is brotherhood the real key to the triple gospel of the idea of humanity. The union of liberty and equality can only be achieved by the power of human brotherhood and it cannot be founded on anything else . . . When the soul claims freedom, it is the freedom of its self-development, the self-development of the Divine in man in all his being. When it claims equality, what it is claiming is that freedom equally for all and the recognition of the same soul, the same godhead in all human beings. When it strives for brotherhood, it is founding that equal freedom for self-development on a common aim, a common life, a unity of mind and feeling founded upon the recognition of this inner spiritual unity. These three things are in fact the nature of the soul; for freedom, equality, unity, are the eternal attributes of the spirit. It is the practical recognition of this truth, it is the awakening of the soul in man and the attempt to get him to live from his soul and not from his ego which is the inner meaning of religion, and it is that to which the religion of humanity also must arrive before it can fulfil itself in the life of the race.*

Paramahansa Yogananda:[2]

> *But although high in intellectual attainments, many Westerners are caught up in rank materialism . . .*
>
> *East and West must now establish a golden middle path, of action wedded to spirituality.*

Rudolf Steiner:[3,4]

> *What one could compare individual countries to, at the most, would be cells of an organism; as an economic body, the entire world can only be compared to an organism. We have to take note of this. Ever since we have had a world economy, it is much easier to understand that individual countries can only be compared to cells. The whole Earth considered as an economic organism, is the (actual) social organism . . .*
>
> *You will only be able to understand the book [Towards Social Renewal, GA 23] if you begin to understand why even the best organized things won't work if you have to depend on people whose minds are blocked by traditional thinking. Above all else, these minds will have to be filled with other ideas. What, then, is the real challenge? You have to advocate a new mode of holistic thinking, above all teach people to think in a different way. This is the call each of you can respond to: ensure that new ideas enlighten people's minds. Instead of elaborating tired programmes that propose short-sighted social reforms, bring a universal perspective to bear on social needs instead, and kindle insight into what is really needed. That is how you convert ideas into practical reality.*

THE BIODYNAMIC FARM AND THE SOCIAL ORGANISM

Programme of the conference, of which the author's talk formed a part:

Save Our Earth as a Healthy Organism
Meeting in Chennai, Amethyst, 23 December 2012, 10.30 am

Song for the World—Save Our Earth as a Healthy Organism

10.30 h Musical Introduction Musica Mundi—Contemplations on a Culture of Sound: Explorations, Improvisations, Compositions with various natural instruments, voice, flute, viola
by Aurelio and Nadaprem (from Auroville and Lithuania)

Introduction by Dr. Lucas Dengel, Secretary of the Biodynamic Association of India, Executive EcoPro, Auroville. Dr. Lucas will facilitate the meeting.

11.00 h 1st speaker: Mother Earth—Care for Nature as Task of the Younger Generation. The School for Biodynamic Farming
Jakes Jayakaran, President of the Biodynamic Association of India, and Founder of the School for Biodynamic Farming in Vinobajipuram (Tamil Nadu)

11.45 h 2nd speaker: What does Biodynamic Farming mean?
Dr. Peter Schaumberger, CEO IMO Switzerland (Institute for Market Ecology), 25 Years Experience in the Organic Industry (Fair Trade Sustainability)

12.30 h Music

13.00 h Lunch Break (snacks available from the buffet)

13.30 h Music

14.00 h 3rd speaker: The Biodynamic Farm and the Social Organism—Practical Concepts for a New World
Ulrich RöEsch, Managing Director of a textile company, social economist and scientist, Germany

14.45 h Discussion with the speakers. Closing words by Dr. Lucas Dengel

15.30 h Music

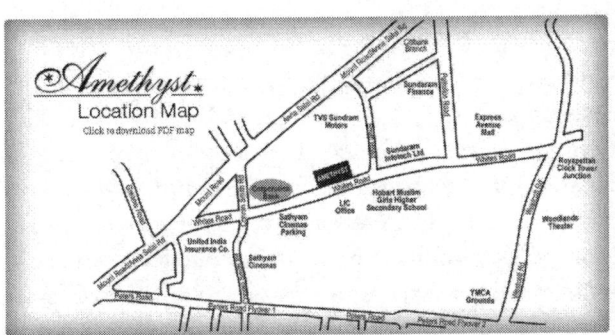

My dear friends, It is a great pleasure to be part of this festival for our earth. We modern people are not very kind to our planet. We hurt our earth. We treat it very impolitely and are unpleasant to it. Of course, our time on earth will come to an end. When he was 90 years old, my wife's beloved teacher once said: I take a walk every day. This is necessary, because I want to be healthy when I die. He meant, that he will have to pass away like every human being, whenever it is time, but he has to take care of his own body in the meantime.

So too, we have to take care of our world, even though the earth will someday become charcoal or even slag, only waste matter; then we will have to reach a new spiritual stage. We can understand our earth to be our own extended physical body. So we have to take care of it, not in an egotistical way, but we are now the caretakers in our time, for our beloved earth. So I am very happy that Aurelio and his colleague have made the wonderful music we just heard. It is not only we few who have heard these tunes—but also the elemental beings in the South and North, in the West and East. And of course they will also be aware of the words spoken here.

When we talk about biodynamic farming, we have to speak about the creator of this new method of living agriculture, Rudolf Steiner (1861–1925). I would like to quote Heimo Rau, the founder of the Max Mueller Bhawan Institutes in India: 'Rudolf Steiner can rightly be called the universal genius of the 20th century.' Steiner brought together science and spirituality—the physical and the metaphysical world. You can find a certain similarity in his contemporary, Sri Aurobindo (1872–1950). For a certain time the Theosophical Society—based in Adyar—offered Rudolf Steiner a forum for his work. In 1902 he became the General Secretary of the German Section of the world association, which was led by Annie Besant.

But Steiner did not accept anything which originated only from an esoteric theosophical tradition he himself had not penetrated with his own spiritual research. For that reason, in 1912 he founded the Anthroposophical Society and he gave very penetrating lectures on *The Occult Foundations of the Bhagavad Gita* (published in English in Bombay, in 1975).

Striving for a new organic picture of society, developing his concepts of the threefold social organism, and establishing a new form of education in Waldorf pedagogy, Steiner devoted himself always to perceive mankind as a wholeness, and not only as an abstraction in his intellect, bound in 'head thinking'. For him, art in all its forms plays a central role in human life. He introduced a movement for social renewal and gave hundreds of talks to help people bring his concepts of a threefold social order into practice. At the end of his life, he gave courses to farmers, peasants and estate owners about a new, organic form of agriculture. Drawing on the experience of our forefathers and modern knowledge of biological science, he combined these with knowledge and wisdom he gained from the spiritual world to create biodynamic agriculture.

We are very happy to now have the Biodynamic Association of India with its President Jakes Jayakaran and its Secretary Dr. Lucas Dengel. Thank you for making this event possible.

1. Introduction: the curse of neoliberalism

Before talking about the biodynamic farm and the social organism, I must first speak of our whole earth as a social organism. We live in one world— we are one world. 'The whole earth, considered as an economic organism, is the social organism.'[5] With these words Rudolf Steiner opened his course on World Economy in July 1922 in Dornach. This was at a time when modern economic theory had already started to talk about 'national economy'. Steiner was ahead of his time. So we must always start with the whole world, the earth as a totality, when we want to talk about any social issue.

I found a long interview with Jean Ziegler, a very committed Swiss citizen—a politician, a professor of sociology, a diplomat and a representative of the United Nations. He travelled around the world on behalf of the UN to do research and to proclaim the human right to sufficient nourishment. He stated that every child who dies of hunger has been murdered. The UN world report on famine says that we could easily feed 12 billion people. Ziegler writes:

> The murdering mechanisms are man-made. For that reason people could change them, too. The countries from which the murderous 'trusts' come are democracies! There is no lack of awareness. People can do anything. We can change our social world... Yes, of course the average income in India has increased tremendously. But according to the FAO, half of Indian children still suffer from severe malnutrition. The increase in national average income has not addressed malnutrition in the country ... This is the curse of neoliberalism ... The biggest companies have more power than any king, any emperor or pope in former times.[6]

Everywhere in the world, between 1 and 2 per cent of people own 70–80 per cent of the land ... and the majority of people suffer. I think it is our task to change this world. Every day that we tolerate the old system increases our guilt.

2. Creating economic values

Let us now look at the social organism, and let's practise Rudolf Steiner's scientific method in the Goethean sense by looking at the subject in its totality, as a whole. He gathers together all the effects, all the impressions that he perceives. In this way he assembles a work of art, and in this composed totality the spectator can also experience the essence, the inner being of what is being observed. In the beginning one may not understand all parts of this composition, but we may use them as signposts to find our way to the spirit, to the inner essence of phenomena. We perceive the phenomenon as it appears in the world, such that its concept, its lawfulness, its idea can be brought to expression within cognitive thinking. In the first step towards understanding economic values, Rudolf Steiner describes it thus:

> An economic value, seen from this one aspect, is a natural product transformed by human labour... One value-forming factor is human labour, which transforms a natural product so as to introduce it into economic circulation ...

Then comes a second aspect:

> Here we have the second aspect of value-forming factors in economics. Here labour stands in the background, and before it the spirit which directs and governs the labour. Labour shines through the spirit, and this again creates an economic value.[7]

I would like to explain some fundamental economic facts. I do hope I shall not bore you. Economics can be very tiresome and irksome. But done in the right life-exploring way, it can be very exciting.

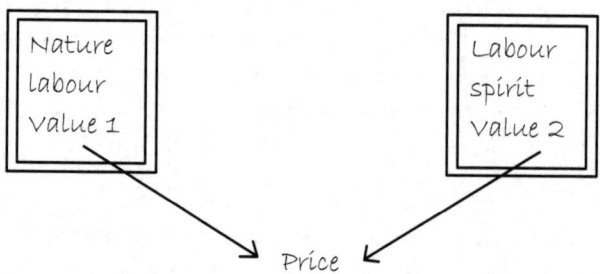

In value 1 we have 'labour applied to nature' and in value 2, 'spirit applied to labour'. This means, in the first case, that labour is directing the process of transforming nature, giving rise to economic value 1; and in the second case, spirit directs and transforms labour, thus creating economic value 2.

Rudolf Steiner gives us a very important and precise description of work:

> Work, in the economic sense, begins when human beings produce for one another... Work arises when nature is transformed by the human being for the purpose of being consumed... Work is a human activity expended on a natural product to render it consumable... By (means of) intelligence one can share out this work, but the resulting structuring of work distances itself from the product. It is a mere division of labour.[8]

This makes it very clear that only work done for the needs of consumers is work in the sense illustrated in Rudolf Steiner's economics course. And it also shows that the directing of work can be a purely spiritual deed, manifesting in the labour applied to transforming matter.

We find the three factors of production:

$$\text{Nature—Labour—Spirit (capital).}$$

Steiner speaks of the 'loan character of industrial capital'.

We find these elements are related to the concepts of:

$$\text{purchase—loans—gifts}$$

as well as:

$$\text{commodities—means of production—industrial capital}$$

Here Rudolf Steiner observes the step, the metamorphosis, that occurs between a bartering economy to a money economy, and a further metamorphosis to arrive at an economy of human faculties (abilities). This economy of faculties is where we actually find ourselves today, but our thinking and our concepts still remain in the past, corresponding to the structure of a bartering economy.

The essential point is that we have a new structure in the economic realm: the production side and the consumption side have developed into a polarity. This polarity highlights two different processes and concepts for the production side and the consumption side. The concepts we use in our economic life still belong to the time before and of Adam Smith (1723–1790), concepts built up in relation to a barter economy, including concepts of private property, which are only adequate for the one side, that of the private domain of the consumer. In the realm of production in modern times, with its elaborated division of labour, it makes no sense to speak of property, whether private, collective or mutual. The means of production are part of the total system of production, and the individual or group with the best capacities or faculties uses them to produce what it creates for other people. To be healthy, an economy of faculties has to enable the means of production to keep moving around to the person or the group with the best faculties and mode of application.

And this is the most decisive task for entrepreneurial activity: to direct capital to the individual or the group with the best capability and efficiency. For land property it is the same. You may see that we have to go beyond what is known today as capitalism. But we have to explore a new freedom.

Let's look at the quote from Sri Aurobindo in the invitation to our programme today [see above]:

> *The aim of the religion of humanity was formulated in the eighteenth century by a sort of primal intuition; that aim was and it is still to recreate human society in the image of three kindred ideas: liberty, equality and fraternity. None of these has really been won in spite of all the progress that has been achieved ... It has laboured to establish a political, social and legal liberty, equality and mutual help in an equal association.*

It is not easy to understand and practise this Goethean path of cognition and its phenomenological method, but by doing so we can experience freedom in knowing and action illumined by a thinking methodology that is entirely modern and, in my view, extremely valuable. But a second step has to be added when we approach the social realm. A large enough number of people must come into association with each other if they want to change conditions in the world. Our world urgently needs to change to safeguard humanity's continuing survival. So let us seek to practise this new approach to thinking, and let us join together in social groups that are willing to work towards a new world: let us **create living social sculpture together**.

3. The biodynamic farm as an organism

Biodynamic work always seeks wholeness. The biodynamic farm itself creates its own organism. And if we look at the farm as a social organism, we can see that the farm organism finds its place in the polarity between the cosmos and the earth.

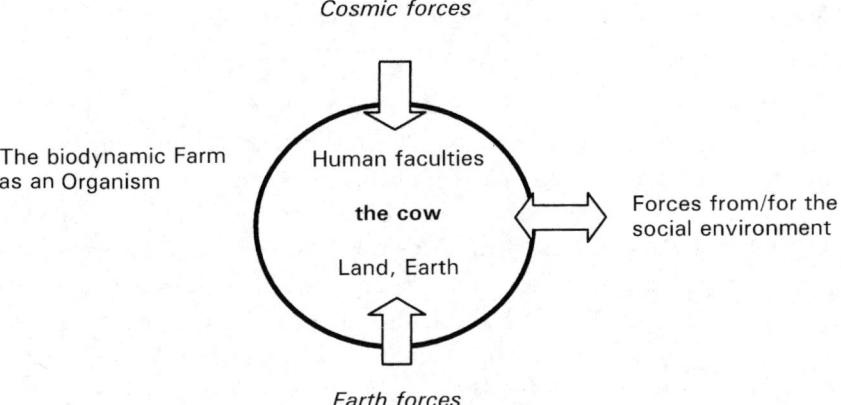

And of course the cow stands at the centre of the farm; in India people know that the cow is the centre of our earthly existence or even the centre of the cosmos. We receive the divine milk from the cow; we see the repeated chewing, her infinite gaze towards eternity, and can't forget the valuable cow dung, the nourishment for our fields. And the fact that cosmic forces affect the earth was very clear to our forefathers. They asked their Brahmins before they sowed their fields or worked with nature, if the constellation of the planets, the stars, was propitious. We have talked about the farm organism, the social organism as a whole, and of the economic organism. One cannot be understood without the other. An inner view of the phenomena always includes the wholeness, the totality.

Social organism ⇔ Farm organism ⇔ Economic organism

4. The threefold social organism

Between the earth and our spiritual work, we have the task of developing our own social organism, which can now be consciously created by human beings. And then we can see how the good spiritual forces shaped our social organism as a threefold one. The Christian tradition of course knows threefoldness in the Trinity. In Hinduism we also have three divine forces: Brahma the Creator, Vishnu the preserver and Shiva the destroyer.

As human beings we are born as members of a family, a social community, a caste and so on. Our physical organization is dependent upon the laws of heredity. We belong to our parents as well as to a specific society and community. But our talents and abilities are intimately bound up with our individual karma. It is our most sacred duty to train and develop our abilities. Rudolf Steiner said that our talents and abilities are the fruits of learning in past lives:

> A physical body makes its appearance, having received its form through the laws of heredity. This body becomes the vehicle for a spirit that is repeating an earlier life in a new form. Between the two, living a self-contained life of its own, stands the soul. The soul is what actually embeds us in this earthly life. Through the body, we belong to the physical human genus; we are members of this genus. With our spirit, we live in a higher world. The soul binds the two worlds together for a while. The course of a human life within the framework of life and death is determined in three different ways, and we are therefore also dependent on three factors that go beyond birth and death. The body is subject to the laws of heredity; the soul is subject to self-created destiny or, to use an ancient term, to its karma; and the spirit is subject to the laws of reincarnation, or repeated earthly lives.[9]

Thus our first link to the social organism is our spiritual life, which is essentially founded upon human abilities or capacities. These include not only our most important achievements at a mundane level, but everything born out of the spiritual or physical abilities acquired by humankind. A human being who does something with his hands gains skill by practising. Every human being thus takes part in the social realm of the spiritual life. The first realm in social life is the spiritual life; this is the area where human faculties become developed, so they can be applied to another sphere. They become part of a person's individual abilities. These are constantly growing as the individual human being evolves.

The second realm of the social organism is the economic life. In the economic realm we are only dealing with production, consumption and the movement of goods and commodities. A product that achieves value for a customer within the context of his or her social relationships will eventually result in a certain price for the product, and this will transform the product into a commodity. In this second area of the social organism an understanding and an agreement between producer and consumer is needed. To find a valid judgement in the area of economic life, a collective judgement must be arrived at through a process of communication within the community.

Between these two realms, the spiritual and the economic, a third is found: it is the area where a human being encounters another human being. This middle area is of a purely human nature. And it embraces all relationships in which an individual opens up towards another human being: not as an economic subject, not as a gifted genius, but as a human being, as a fellow citizen. In this realm of rights between human beings we are only dealing with entitlement and obligation or commitment. This is the third, or middle realm of the social organism—the rights life, or life of the state.

There is another threefold situation if we look at the market:

producer   **distributer**   **consumer**

Together, they have to find **fair, righteous prices**.

And again Rudolf Steiner made us aware of a very important polarity. Economy starts with the abilities of the human being, transforming a given part of nature into a consumable product (see Chapter 2), and this develops into an ever more sophisticated production process, guided and created by the human spirit.

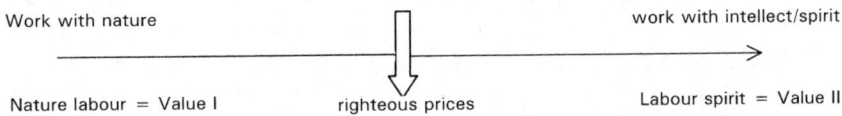

Work with nature → work with intellect/spirit

Nature labour = Value I   righteous prices   Labour spirit = Value II

Rudolf Steiner gave 14 lectures on the theme of how to determine the right price for a commodity. And most of these lectures end by saying this: now we can pursue this theme no further. This is because going further is the task of new groups, of a future economy of fraternity and solidarity. So, important steps towards this new economy will begin with associations in which consumers join together with producers; and this task will be mediated by distributers. In today's economy there is a polarity between producers and consumers. This polarity has to be overcome.

Conclusion

We talked about the farm organism, the social organism as a whole and the economic organism. One cannot be understood without the other. We have to develop a new living thinking and we have to develop a healthy will to create the world in which we want to live. Only working together actively in this way will we create the future that we want.

The agriculture course given by Rudolf Steiner in 1924 ends by giving thanks to the good forces in world evolution that allowed the course to take place, made it into a great festival, a celebratory event in world history. May this meeting here in Chennai also become such a celebration.

Thank you Jayakaran, thank you Dr. Lucas, thank you Dr. Schaumberger, thanks to the musicians and thank you to all who made this conference possible.

Notes

1. Sri Aurobindo, *The Ideal of Human Unity*, Pondicherry 1919, pp. 545–547.
2. Paramahansa Yogananda, *Autobiography of a Yogi*, Second Indian Edition, 1975, Jaico Publishing House, Bombay.
3. Rudolf Steiner, *World Economy*, lecture 1, 24.7.1922, GA 340.
4. Rudolf Steiner, 'Impulses of the past and future for social life', GA 190.
5. Rudolf Steiner, *World Economy*, Rudolf Steiner Press, London 1977.
6. *Basler Zeitung*, 18.9.2012.
7. Rudolf Steiner, *World Economy*, London 1972, Rudolf Steiner Press, pp. 31–32.

    Editor's note: *Labour shines through the spirit* refers directly to an example that Rudolf Steiner gave a moment before in the lecture, describing how a background colour can be overlaid by another colour but will still shine through it—showing something of itself, but changed by what now covers it. Thus spirit overlays labour, and labour now shines through that spirit, as if from beneath it, expressing itself in a new way, in a new hue.
8. Rudolf Steiner, 'Discourses' in *Economics*, GA 341, New Economy Publications, p. 209.
9. Rudolf Steiner, *Theosophy*, GA 9, Anthroposophic Press 1994, pp. 83–89.